HOW
CLASSICAL POETRY

A Guide to Forms, Techniques, and Meaning

The Society of Classical Poets

Mount Hope, New York

CONTENTS

About the Society

TODAY, POETRY is everywhere. It is in the songs on the radio, in our national anthems, and in the fight songs of our favorite sports teams; it pervades our literature, our history, and our culture. But, despite poetry's abundance, poetry that is both new and good is hard to find now, more than ever. Good, new poetry cherishes and builds on the perennial forms, like meter and rhyme, left to us by 1,400 years of English poets, who have also built on thousands of years of Greek, Japanese, and Chinese poetry. Such good, new poetry carries a message infused with the profound insights and lofty character of the poet. It touches on humanity's quintessential quest for virtue over vice, epic over ephemeral, and beauty over baseness.

With this in mind, the Society of Classical Poets is a 501(c)(3) non-profit organization formed in 2012 as a group of poets dedicated to the revival and proliferation of good, new poetry.

The Society's mission is to preserve humankind's artistic traditions; to reestablish poetry as one of the most widely appreciated forms of literature, communication, and entertainment; to increase appreciation of centuries of rhyming or metered poetry; to support poets who apply classical techniques in modern poetry through publication and performance opportunities and awards; and to advance language arts in education and culture.

A Brief Introduction

THIS IS A book about writing poetry, specifically classical poetry. If we go back 100 years or so, then the 1,300 years of English poetry before that was all classical poetry and it was just called poetry. So, we might have called this book simply "How to Write Poetry" or "How to Write Real Poetry," but for clarity's sake, we have opted for "Classical Poetry."

Chapter 1 of this book deals with why poetry is still great and useful in our modern world. When we get down to literature at its most beautiful, profound, and memorable, it is often in the form of poetry. In this chapter, we visit those places where poetry has succeeded and continues to succeed throughout the English-speaking world today. The last section of this chapter includes four poems and 25 Advanced Placement (AP) level questions useful for high school English classes.

Chapter 2 deals with the detailed mechanics of how to write poetry and how to write specific poetry forms, such as the sonnet, the haiku, the limerick, and so on. Of course, one does not need a form to write poetry. We give the nuts and bolts without any form in Section 2.3, but forms can be useful and certainly provide excellent practice. The book's name is derived from Chapter 2—this is a how-to book. There are classical and contemporary examples in almost every section of this chapter. Many of these sections are written by different authors, so the expression of ideas and notations might not be uniform. We have left it this way on purpose: It is meant to give different dimensions to the art of poetry, just as a degree in a particular discipline entails learning from different professors.

It is crucial to note that the mechanics in Chapter 2 deal mostly with the surface form of poetry. You could perfectly master the mechanics and still write a terrible poem, just as a speaker may correctly read every word of a speech but not move his or her audience because of the dry and unenthusiastic tone; a restaurant may have great waiters and beautiful ambience but terrible food, a violinist may play all the correct notes but sound dull, and so on. The ultimate key to greatness in poetry is the feeling or inner beauty behind the external form.

What sort of feeling should a great poem have? This is where Chapter 3 on great poetry of the past comes into play. By studying and appreciating those great poems of the past, one can begin to understand the intangible requirements for writing poetry well. Specifically, poetry should strive to be exquisitely beautiful, delightfully entertaining, and boldly engaging. Meanwhile, it also must reinforce, or at least not subtract from, those basic moral standards that fortify and enhance rich cultures and lasting civilizations. That is great poetry.

1. WHY POETRY IS GREAT

W
H
Y
?

by Evan Mantyk

1.1 The Power of Praise

IN THE CLASSICAL traditions and history of every human culture, there was a belief in the divine and a deep reverence for it. This gave rise to poems or songs of praise, such as hymns, odes, and paeans. Today, praise of this kind is relatively uncommon outside of religions, but praise, celebration, and honor nonetheless continue unabated.

Let's say you like something or someone and you want to tell the world, "Hey, you're great," or "I admire that," or "That thing looked so cool!" but you want to express it in some way that is more meaningful than those plain words. If that is the case, then poetry may hold the key. With very little materials needed, you can create a small artistic monument to whatever it is that has so moved you. It may be brilliant or it may be terrible, but undeniably it is special and captures something between you and it.

We begin with poems from the famous 19th-century Poet Laureate of Great Britain, Lord Alfred Tennyson, and the greatest American poet of the 20th century, Robert Frost. Then we move on to three living poets who write in the style of classical poetry. In each, the poet praises his subject matter, and tries to capture what it is that moved him in unique ways.

The Eagle

by Lord Alfred Tennyson (1809–1892)

He clasps the crag with crooked hands;
Close to the sun in lonely lands,
Ringed with the azure world, he stands.

The wrinkled sea beneath him crawls;
He watches from his mountain walls,
And like a thunderbolt he falls.

A Passing Glimpse

by Robert Frost (1874–1963)

I often see flowers from a passing car
That are gone before I can tell what they are.

I want to get out of the train and go back
To see what they were beside the track.

I name all the flowers I am sure they weren't:
Not fireweed loving where woods have burnt—

Not bluebells gracing a tunnel mouth—
Not lupine living on sand and drouth.*

Was something brushed across my mind
That no one on earth will ever find?

Heaven gives its glimpses only to those
Not in position to look too close.

The Winter Solstice

by Neal Dachstadter

Winter, Winter, cold and crass.
Winter, Winter, old the grass.
Fast we go across the field,
Massed the snow and frost to wield.
Night of rest abed when tired
Light and fest and sled and fire.

---

* Archaic form of the word "drought": a long period of time during which there is very little or no rain.

Bubbles

by Michael Dashiell

I swish the stick
To watch a spread of bubbles gleam;
Free and delightful they float
Almost a dream.

This pristine orbs,
A fragile yet audacious batch
Seem hopeless until they reveal
A rainbow patch.

They move away
And occupy a placid realm
To demonstrate the physics of
Cohesive film.

I notice soon
A strange geography revealed,
A surface spin of nations or
Plasmatic field.

Expectancy
That this existent play will stop
Makes any conclusion forgone
These orbs must pop.

As lovely eyes
They dare not recognize or wink
Because if excited they're gone
Quick as a blink.

I stand and watch
Their glorious defeat, yet one
That wanders, hesitates then bursts
Succeeds to stun.

On Seeing Shen Yun Performing Arts

a rondeau

by Evan Mantyk

I love the dance that can exalt
The human form without a fault,
Demeanor grand, inspiring pose;
They're swift yet seem in sweet repose

And all my troubled thoughts they halt.
Then when as one they somersault
It's like a mighty thunderbolt;
My heart entranced then clearly knows
I love the dance.

Their order raised from life's tumult
Does with a higher power vault
Above to where true kindness grows
And tolerance like water flows,
And though it's brief, as a result
I love the dance.

For Students
1. List all of the different topics of praise in the above poems. Add three topics that you would praise.
2. Pick one of your topics and list what you like about the topic specifically and in detail. Attempt a four-line poem on the topic.

1.2 Humor Elevated

FROM MOTHER GOOSE to Dr. Seuss, rhyme has induced laughter in children century after century. The enchantment of rhyme loses none of its magic on the richly imaginative minds of the young and can still make an adult or two chuckle.

In the first poems below, Nivedita Karthik, an ethnically Indian graduate in integrated immunology from the University of Oxford, in England, offers two Irish limericks that show that rhyming humor works across cultures.

Two Limericks

by Nivedita Karthik

There once was a very young rat
who thought himself a big, black bat.
    So, he leapt off a chair
    and flew through the air
Straight into the jaws of a cat!

The gown and the date are set,
caterers and florists I've met.
    The hall has been booked,
    no detail overlooked
Wait … I don't have a groom just yet!

But, beyond these short limericks, there is a great deal of potential in rhyme as a source of humor beyond what writers today generally imagine. Observe, for instance, Edmond Rostand's 1897 classic work *Cyrano de Bergerac*, which is written entirely in rhyming verse and hilariously pits the unusually large-nosed titular French protagonist against himself and fate. (The 1990 French film adaptation with Gérard Depardieu is recommended.) Some of this ingenious rhyming potential can be seen here in the next poem, by Joshua Lefkowitz. Mr. Lefkowitz was a finalist for the 2014 Brooklyn

Non-Fiction Prize and has also recorded humor pieces for NPR's *All Things Considered* and the BBC's *Americana*.

Insomnia

by Joshua Lefkowitz

When I struggle for sleep,
I dust off a classic
and try counting sheep:

Trouble is, my sheep show off,
they leap like Olympians
over their feeding trough—

They soar through the air,
blending into the clouds,
pirouette, land back down, where

the rest of the animals wait,
giving scores, mostly tens,
'cept the East German pigs, 9.8.

It's all rather amusing, only
I'm still awake, while you doze
by my side, and thus lonely

I nudge you and whisper, "Hi,"
to the which you groan, and reply,
"If you don't shut up, you will die."

In Lefkowitz's poem, what would otherwise be only a well-written and humorous anecdote is elevated to the level of art.

While one is humorously rhyming, there is also the potential to make serious social statements in unique ways. The following is an example of such by British poet and motivational expert James Sale:

Obi-Wan Bin Laden RIP

by James Sale

Let's remember what God wants:
Killing people's never right,
So Obi-Wan Bin Laden then
Cannot be a Jedi knight.

To make folks free you face them straight—
Backstabbing lacks God's protocol;
So Obi-Wan Bin Laden looks
Like something that has lost its soul.

He's hard to find on Dagobah,
Afghanistan or Alderon,
Where Obi-Wan Bin Laden hides—
But surely he'll slip in the sun.

Then see his shade evaporate,
His loud excuses miss their course:
As Obi-Wan Bin Laden tries
Escaping but without the Force.

The use of *Star Wars* allusions and metaphors to talk about a mass-murdering terrorist, Osama bin Laden, may seem, if not humorous, then strange at first, but when you think about it, it makes complete sense. How many troubled Muslim youth being raised today are the terrorists of tomorrow and are dangerously confusing good and evil? Thus, all at once, the poem delivers a necessary social message, a humorous satire, and effective rhyming poetry.

For Students
1. Which poem was most effective for you? Why?
2. Write your own joke, or short humorous story.

1.3 Love Poems

IT IS NO surprise that if you start typing into Google "poems about..." the first phrase that comes up is "poems about love." It is also no surprise that poets are known for romanticizing (idealizing or glorifying) their subject matter, and the words "romance" and "romanticize" today are most often associated with heart-shaped boxes of chocolates, flowers, and all sorts of Valentine's Day merchandise. Poetry, from Shakespeare's sonnets to Lord Byron's *Don Juan* to the lyrics of many a love song today, cannot be disentwined from the sweet and gooey topic of love, nor, many a love bird would say, should it be.

To give some idea of the breadth of such love poetry, I offer love birds a few love poems for almost any situation: The first poem, by the great Romantic-era poet Percy Bysshe Shelley, is perfect if you are shy. Shelley is forward enough for centuries of wooing. The second, by living poet Reid McGrath of Pawling, New York, is perfect for the new love interest. The third poem, by living poet Joseph Charles MacKenzie of New Mexico, is perfect for the happily married. In the 12th line, you might swap out "a poet's wife" to suit your need, for example "a programmer's wife." The last, by living poet Amy Foreman of Arizona, is long but perfect for relationships on the rocks.

Let the wooing commence!

Love's Philosophy

by Percy Bysshe Shelley (1792–1822)

The fountains mingle with the river
And the rivers with the ocean,
The winds of heaven mix for ever
With a sweet emotion;
Nothing in the world is single;
All things by a law divine
In one spirit meet and mingle.
Why not I with thine?—

See the mountains kiss high heaven
And the waves clasp one another;
No sister-flower would be forgiven
If it disdained its brother;
And the sunlight clasps the earth
And the moonbeams kiss the sea:
What is all this sweet work worth
If thou kiss not me?

Valentine

by Reid McGrath

I didn't know when Valentine's Day was,
and didn't need to. That day came and went
like any other. Now I know it 'cause
you're perfect, dear; you don't know what you've meant
to me, my life, completely ignorant
to Love which waters a lush Happiness,
as if my rose-like heart were pinched and pent
up in my dry yet sunless parchéd chest.
You have refreshed; you irrigate my heart.
You're water and you're sunshine and you're air
that's unpolluted: cool then warm. You part
the darkness of my isolated lair.
    Now fertile is my chest; and a Love grows,
    and now you are my Heart; you are my Rose.

For Elizabeth

by Joseph Charles MacKenzie

If charm were a country, then you would be
Its capital of many domes and spires
Gilded and gleaming off a crystal sea,
And graced with every art that love inspires.
If beauty a nation, then you, its queen,
Would wield the scepter of love's dazzling power
Beguiling all thy subjects with serene
And regal allure from a silver tower.
Alas, the fairest flowers remain unknown
Behind the garden walls of married life;
And thou, the loveliest, shouldst not bemoan
The humble title of a poet's wife:
To capitals yet made these lines proclaim
Eternal love, and gild thy beauty's fame.

Ballad: Our Crew of Two

by Amy Foreman

When we set forth, the breeze blew fair,
  The sun shone balmy, warm.
Our sheets were fixed; sail filled with air,
  No warning of the storm.

Our crew of two, so cheerfully,
  With confidence untried,
Thought we could lick the strongest sea
  And still enjoy the ride.

In dinghy small, in ocean great,
  Our tiny course still true.
We charted stars to navigate;
  From Heaven took our cue.

And so we cruised for many years,
  Successful in our tour.
With frequent laughter, scarcer tears,
  The partnership secure.

But one night when the stars were gone
  And clouds obscured our view,
A gust surprised us, struck head-on
  And blew the mast askew.

In darkness thick, with rising surge,
  We struggled with the sail.
The waves now threatened to submerge
  Our vessel in the gale.

We could not see to douse or reef
  And so we grappled, blind;
Our crew of two, in disbelief
  Left buoyancy behind.

The dinghy tossed like wreckage now
  And, hope so far from sight,

We tried once more and then, somehow,
  Our crew began to fight.

Through foam and froth and swelling wave
  Our agitation grew.
Each violent blast a cause to rave,
  To quarrel, stage a coup.

Our crew of two, now one-on-one,
  Not just against the squall
Attacked each other 'til undone,
  A rebel's free-for-all.

So will we drown in waters vast
  This tempest take our souls?
And, sinking, will we still lambaste
  Each other's weak controls?

Or could we, if we changed our tack
  And pulled together, firm,
Outlast this storm, this inky black,
  Our partnership affirm?

Oh, please, let's try, although the sky
  Above is dire and grim.
You take an oar and so will I,
  Together scull and skim.

I'll call you "Captain"; call me "Mate."
  We'll rally, make amends.
And, crew of two, we'll navigate
  This stormy night as friends.

For Students
1. Which love poem do you feel is most effective? Why?
2. Choosing the same situation as one of the poems, write a love letter or poem.

1.4 Riddles

IN ONE OF the tensest moments in J.R.R. Tolkien's *The Hobbit,* Gollum is ready to eat Bilbo Baggins if he cannot answer this riddle correctly:

> Alive without breath,
> As cold as death;
> Never thirsty, ever drinking,
> All in scales but never clinking.*

There is something strange and mysterious about riddles by their very nature, like entering a maze in someone else's mind. Poetry, too, has a strange and mysterious quality by its very nature as an art form springing almost completely from someone's mind and with little intermediary media needed—just pencil and paper, or not even that if you memorize it. Thus, poetry is the ideal method for delivering a riddle.

The rhyming riddle tradition goes back at least as far as ancient Greece. According to some versions of the legend, people would go to the Oracle at Delphi with important questions and she would give an answer that was transcribed into a riddle-like poem. For instance, the King of Lydia, Croesus, fearing the invasion of the King of Persia, Cyrus, went to the Oracle at Delphi to inquire as to whether he should attack before being attacked. He received this answer:

> One day, when a mule shall mount upon the Median throne,
> Then, and not till then, shall great Croesus fear to lose his own.

Croesus took the idea of a mule ruling a kingdom to be an impossibility and thus his chances of losing to be an impossibility. Well, to make a long story short, Croesus got this riddle wrong. He attacked and eventually lost. His enemy, Cyrus, was of mixed blood and was thus represented by the mule (which is a cross between a donkey and horse).

---

* All riddle answers can be found at the end of this section.

Such poetic riddles are not limited to European culture alone. In traditional Chinese culture, it is a custom to answer riddles, often poetic, during the Mid-Autumn Festival, a traditional Chinese holiday. In the great classic Chinese novel from the Qing Dynasty *The Dream of the Red Chamber,* by Cao Xueqin, the following poetic riddles, among others, appear. See if you can figure them out:

The demons flee when I arrive;
My voice is like the thunder's roar
And strikes such fear in all alive,
But now I'm merely ash on floor.

—

The children playing outside look at sky,
To where I glide upon the beauty bright,
And when you lose ahold I'm left to fly
Off: lonely soul of which you'll lose all sight.

—

If you point me south, I'll make it go north
And point me north, I'll make it south go forth.
If this makes you sad, I'll be sad as well,
So smile at me, in happiness we'll dwell.

—Cao Xueqin (1715–1763)

Coming now to the present, after centuries, even millennia, of poetic riddles, the tradition remains delightful:

Some of gold. Some cold like stone.
No wood, no chimney. Yet four rooms
With naught an inch to roam.
Still, where it is. There is home.

—Michelle Tamara Simon

I can be hard to find, even when close by.
If you need a fix, I'm your guy.
You'll see right through me,
When you look into my eye.
Who or What am I?

Hidden in your closet
Sits a calcium deposit,
Gutless but not spineless,
Supportive, and yet mindless.

—Mike Munsell

My mirror image never is that far,
I have five different points just like a star,
While I've no mouth or tongue that I employ,
I make a sound quite loud when struck with joy.
—

Turn me upside down, I'm right side up
Empty out my glass, you fill my cup,
Always I'm on time and never late,
Never am I backwards at any rate.
—

My face is on a U.S. bill you've spent,
But I am not a U.S. president,
My skin is fairer than most that you've seen,
Though badly I was burned in 1814.
—

I am the master of the four great seasons,
Who turns off summer storms for my own reasons,
Who pulls the strings and blows the mighty winds—
Such power, three hundred years could not rescind.

—Evan Mantyk

For Students
1. What sort of situation do you think would fit a poetic riddle?
2. Try to write your own riddle without worrying about poetry or
rhyming. Start from an object and then describe the object's unique
qualities. Go back and try to turn it into a poem once you are done.

Riddle Answers: Tolkien: Fish; Xueqin: Firecracker, Kite, Mirror; Simon: Heart;
Munsell: Needle, Skeleton; Mantyk: Hand, Hourglass, White House, Antonio Vivaldi
(and his *Four Seasons*)

1.5 Music Behind Words

"FOUR SCORE AND seven years ago ..." Even if you can't tell me where these six words come from, there is a good chance that you recognize them. But why? They do not offer wisdom or a witty saying; they are just numbers.

In fact, you remember this phrase because of the music behind the words. The phrase falls into a simple rhythm, the iambic, which is often mimicked in poetry.

An iamb is a pair of syllables, or sound units, with the first syllable being unstressed and the second stressed. (For more on what exactly a syllable is and what stress is, see pages 59-60.)

In the opening words to President Abraham Lincoln's "Gettysburg Address," there are four iambs (stressed syllables in bold, italicized, and underlined): 1. four *__score__*; 2. And *__sev__*; 3. en *__years__*; 4. a*__go__*. It is subtle, but the persistence of these rather meaningless six words in my brain and yours is compelling evidence of the power of musical language.

This is just like the famous Shakespearean quote "To *__be__* or *__not__* to *__be__*, that *__is__* the *__ques__*tion" (with the addition of a soft syllable at the end), and innumerable catchy phrases and idioms; "the *__best__* laid *__plans__* of *__mice__* and *__men__*," or "*__When__* in *__Rome__*, do *__as__* the *__Ro__*mans" (which reverses the stress order of the iambs).

Here we'll look at some classical poems that draw on this enchanting musical power to render beauty in ways that are not only enjoyable but also inspiring. They may even help you write your next greeting card message or Facebook post. The selected poems are written about music, but musical-sounding words theoretically can be used on any topic—even death and war, as President Lincoln showed.

These poems must be read aloud for you to hear the music—preferably to a room of rapt spectators, but by yourself is fine too.

We begin with an excerpt of an exceptionally musical poem by the great Romantic-era American poet Edgar Allan Poe (1809–1849). Here, Poe uses the reverse of an iamb, called the trochee, with the first syllable being stressed and the second unstressed. He uses this and many other techniques to create a poem that seems to dance off the page.

The Bells (First Stanza)

by Edgar Allan Poe (1809–1849)

Hear the sledges with the bells—
Silver bells!
What a world of merriment their melody foretells!
How they tinkle, tinkle, tinkle,
In the icy air of night!
While the stars that oversprinkle
All the heavens, seem to twinkle
With a crystalline delight;
Keeping time, time, time,
In a sort of Runic rhyme,
To the tintinnabulation that so musically wells
From the bells, bells, bells, bells,
Bells, bells, bells—
From the jingling and the tinkling of the bells.

Next is a poem by living poet Don Shook, a writer, actor, director, and producer who formerly worked for NBC in New York. His poem brings to life Beethoven's final and greatest symphony, written after the legendary composer had already gone deaf.

Paean to "Ode to Joy"

by Don Shook

I heard the "Ode to Joy" today,
    ten thousand times at least.
I could not hold my heart at bay,
    engorging on a feast
of melody, of majesty,
    of rhythmic palpitations,
while soaring in full harmony
    with Heaven's exaltations.
The clustered chords embraced my soul,
    sustaining strains sublime
of resonance beyond control
    above the staff of time.

Celestial voices raised the theme
   in joy that did inspire
a cadence that would surely seem
   born of the inner fire
of he who could not hear one note
   with which he could discern
the artistry, that as he wrote,
   past tribulations spurned.
The "Ode" exploded with the might
   Beethoven had released
and blessed the earth with such delight
   perversion's rapture ceased.
I heard the "Ode to Joy" today,
   ten thousand times too few.

Finally, we have a sonnet from living poet C.B. Anderson, who was the longtime gardener for the PBS television series *The Victory Garden*. If you listen closely, you'll hear in each line a steady and exquisite rhythm of two soft beats followed by one hard beat, called an anapest. Here is the first line with the hard syllables emphasized: "Just as ***white*** as a ***blan***ket of ***new***-fallen ***snow***."

Water Music

by C.B. Anderson

Just as white as a blanket of new-fallen snow
Is the noise of a waterfall cresting a brim
And ebulliently thrashing the basin below.
But the sound of a freshet resembles a hymn,
Its discrete iterations like chants that were spoke
By the guardian spirits of hillside and dale,
Yet complex, contrapuntal and clearly baroque.
The continuo rain, the percussion of hail
And the basso profundo of groaning black ice
May accompany geysers erupting with steam
To engender a numinous pearl of great price
In the heart of a mind at the edge of a dream.
The symphonic fantasia that water creates
Is a blend of its various physical states.

These compositions are poems about music that sound musical because of their meter. But musical-sounding words can add a new dimension to topics that have nothing to do with music. The following piece is from the ancient Greek poet Homer's *Iliad*, with a superb translation by 18th-century English poet Alexander Pope. As you will hear, his musical language, structured with meter and repetition, has a feeling of movement to it that brings to life the fighting in the half-mythical Trojan War.

Excerpt from Book 4 of *The Iliad*

By Homer (8th century BC?)
/ Translated by Alexander Pope (1688–1744)

Now shield with shield, with helmet helmet closed,
To armor armor, lance to lance opposed,
Host against host with shadowy squadrons drew,
The sounding darts in iron tempests flew,
Victors and vanquished joined unrestrained cries,
And shrilling shouts and dying groans arise;
With streaming blood the slippery fields are dyed,
And slaughtered heroes swell the dreadful tide.
As torrents roll, and streams increase their fill,
With rage impetuous, down their echoing hills.

Last, we have a poem from living Californian poet Lorna Davis, who took second place in the Society of Classical Poets' 2017 Poetry Competition. In this poem, musical words bring to life a very different topic, and the lush rhymes and meter mirror the beauty that can be found in an ordinary day. Note that, similar to "Water Music," the meter here is two soft beats followed by one hard beat, so the first line should be read "As I **mudd**le my **way** through a **reg**ular **day**."

Songs of a Day

by Lorna Davis

As I muddle my way through a regular day,
   And my feeling of weariness grows,
I am riddled with blue in an indigo hue
   And a dark fog around me that shows.
But my garden is where I can work in fresh air,
   And my blues turn a rosier shade;
As I clip and I rake, with each breath that I take,
   All that dullness inside starts to fade.

And the song of my heart bubbles up like a spring,
And my shadows are lifted and lightly take wing.
As my body starts swaying, I quietly sing
And I feel a connectedness to everything ...

At the dimming of day, as I'm tapping away
   At the keyboard that sits on my desk,
I am caught by the sight of the setting sun's light
   And a view that is quite picturesque.
In that moment I find there's no work in my mind,
   Just the view that is waiting outside,
And I'm crossing the floor to the sliding glass door,
   And I eagerly open it wide.

And the song of my soul rushes in on the breeze
Like the rippling of water and wind in the trees,
And it cleanses my mind as it fills me with ease
Rising up from the ground through my feet and my knees ...

So I head up the hill with a need to fulfill,
   To see more of this glorious sky,
With its crimson and pink, and that spun glass I think
   Must be cirrus clouds streaming up high.
When I get to the top I turn 'round and I stop,
   Stricken dumb by the beauty I see:
Lilac hills touched with green, and a gold sun between
   Slipping into a molten-glass sea.

And the songs of my ancestors hum in my bones,
With sharp clapping rhythms and resonant tones,
With high ululations and deep-throated moans
That sing to the sky and the trees and the stones ...

Strolling back to my house, insignificant mouse
    That I am on this marvelous world,
I am blessed with the sight, as we all are each night,
    Of the stars and the darkness unfurled.
As cerulean blue turns a deep midnight hue,
    I can seek out our faithful North Star,
And as diamonds are spread in the bowl overhead,
    I am struck by how lucky we are.

And the song of the universe tumbles through space
Full of beauty and power, rhythm and grace,
And the light is its voice as it sings through each place
And it spills from the sky to my uplifted face ...

As this day finds its end, I must ponder again
    All that glumness I felt at its start,
And how rarely we see all this real majesty
    That can fill and restore every heart.
And this earth, oh this Earth! The bright world of our birth
    Is a miracle in every way.
As contentment runs deep, I am lulled into sleep
    By the lingering songs of the day.

For Students
1. What saying, quote, or phrase do you know that fits perfectly or
nearly perfectly into a meter pattern, whether it's iambs or trochees?
2. Pick four lines of one of the poems and write them out on a piece
of paper. Then mark the hard syllables by underlining them.

1.6 Advanced Placement English Study

POETRY CONTINUES TO be an excellent training ground for future scholars and leaders, whether literary or not. Just think: There has been virtually no period in history when scholars and leaders were not learning and studying classical poetry. From *The Iliad* and *The Odyssey*, *Beowulf*, and Shakespearean literature in the West to the Chinese *Classic of Poetry*, the Indian *Ramayana*, and the Middle Eastern *Epic of Gilgamesh*, classical poetry is the foundation of literature and education in almost every culture historically.

That spirit continues today in English literature classes throughout the English-speaking world. Here we offer three classical poems written by contemporary poets and an excerpt from Shakespeare's *Merchant of Venice*, which is mostly in the poetry style known as blank verse (unrhymed iambic pentameter). After each poem are questions at the introductory college level, also known as the Advanced Placement (AP) level. Answers are provided at the end of this section. The first poem is a villanelle, a form that you can read more about in the next chapter, on page 65. The third is a sonnet, a form that you can read more about in the next chapter, on page 44.

Apes or Angels

by Ron L. Hodges

Humans, some say, aren't much more than an ape—
A reasoning beast, quintessence of dust.
Others believe we're of angelic shape.

Lines   Hungry for morsels, we scrabble and scrape,
5   Leaving the tree to indulge termite lust.
Humans, some say, aren't much more than an ape.

Yet not all dwell in this feral landscape—
Their minds are free to transcend what hearts must.
Others believe we're of angelic shape.

10   We squat under shadows, covet and rape,
Then flaunt our filth like a Renaissance bust.
Humans, some say, aren't much more than an ape.

Still, there are many whose spirits escape
The region where bodies settle for crust.
15   Others believe we're of angelic shape.

Though such a question makes all skeptics jape,
How could our good rise from matter unjust?
Humans, some say, aren't much more than an ape;
I must believe we're of angelic shape.

1. What is the relationship between the two groups—apes and angels—in the poem?
   (A) They are battling each other in a spiritual war.
   (B) They are two possible ways for human beings to view themselves.
   (C) Both are part of the poet's identity throughout the poem.
   (D) One is depicted as male and the other as female.
   (E) Both groups have similar weaknesses.

2. Which of the following can be concluded about the poet's view of apes?
   (A) Human beings are not like apes.
   (B) Human beings evolved from apes over a long period of time.
   (C) Human beings must try to be like apes.
   (D) Human beings who are skeptical of angels are acting like apes.
   (E) Human beings often act like apes.

3. What is the rhetorical purpose of "jape" in line 16?
   (A) To demonstrate the wisdom of skeptics.
   (B) To highlight how everyone shares a common understanding.
   (C) To emphasize that the question in line 17 may be criticized.
   (D) To clarify the relationship between apes and angels.
   (E) To examine the significance of skeptical questions.

4. Why does the poet mention "Renaissance bust" in line 11?
   (A) To show how filth is treated liked an artistic achievement.
   (B) To suggest that the Renaissance was characterized by coveting and raping.
   (C) To incorporate a modern allusion.
   (D) To question people's use of Renaissance busts.
   (E) To imply that classical art is filth.

5. What best characterizes "scrabble and scrape" in line 4?
   (A) Uncivilized behavior.
   (B) The power of wilderness.
   (C) Anger toward nature.
   (D) Hubris.
   (E) Hard work.

6. What is implied by the poet's use of "must" in line 8?
   (A) What hearts need strength to overcome.
   (B) What hearts aspire toward.
   (C) What hearts are required to follow based on society's rules.
   (D) What hearts do by their nature.
   (E) What hearts have failed at.

The Last Column

Lines inspired by the 9/11 Memorial

by Ron L. Hodges

A shaft of steel rises erect,
its dappled surface all bedecked,
small reminders for all who come
this was and is the last column.

Lines
5   After the soaring spires were wrecked,
into madness the heroes trekked.
Their sacrifice, a gruesome sum,
is blazoned on the last column,

a sight that sears us with respect,
10   a sight that prods us to reflect:
when terror dropped its wicked plumb,
most nobly stood the last column.

But chaos had an architect,
a hate that grows if left unchecked.
15   Still pounding on a martial drum
they vilify the last column.

These tyrants of a hateful sect
both liberty and life reject,
and lest to them our world succumb
20   we must arise, the last column.

7. What is the rhetorical effect of using "rises" in line 1?
    (A) It explains the "gruesome sum" in line 7.
    (B) It acts as a vivid simile.
    (C) It uses the future tense to foretell what will happen.
    (D) It gives movement to an otherwise static object.
    (E) It contradicts the "dappled surface" in line 2.

8. What is the relationship between the first stanza (lines 1–4) and the second stanza (lines 5–8)?
   (A) The second stanza continues the linear chronological story begun in the first stanza.
   (B) The first and second stanzas juxtapose opposing ideas.
   (C) The second stanza limits itself to the imagery used in the first stanza.
   (D) The second stanza provides context to the first stanza.
   (E) The second stanza introduces the last column.

9. What does "architect" in line 13 refer to?
   (A) The designers of the structure.
   (B) The poet himself.
   (C) The destroyers of the building.
   (D) The heroes in line 6.
   (E) The last column.

10. Within the poem, what is "martial drum" in line 15 best described as a metaphor for?
    (A) Troops going to battle.
    (B) A malicious ideology.
    (C) People defending freedom.
    (D) Opposition to Westernization.
    (E) Totalitarian dictators.

11. What does the poet most likely use "last column" in the last line to also refer to?
    (A) The poet himself and the intended audience.
    (B) The last day that the building stood.
    (C) The "tyrants" in line 17.
    (D) The construction of a new column.
    (E) All those who haven't read the poem.

12. Overall, how does the poet develop his theme?
    (A) By examining the effectiveness of an idea.
    (B) By comparing and contrasting two groups of people.
    (C) By traveling to the source of the theme.
    (D) By looking into the past from the present, and reflecting on the future.
    (E) By presenting a solution to an international economic crisis that affects everyone.

The Backwards Romantic

by Reid McGrath

I'm prone to loathe the radio and television, noise
from all angles, laptops, iPads, cellphones—
the gibber-jabber of the wired boys
Lines and girls. I crave the silence of the Stones
  5   of Venice, eerie quiet, sacred sound
that's not quite sound: the wind-chimes' plaintive tune,
the creaking trees in snow, a shrieking loon
on a morning lake where fog and calm abound ...
I'd have preferred a horse-cart out tonight:
  10   with only the yotes yipping and the clop
clop-clottering of horses—by the light
of lantern—who knew when and where to stop
without a map, much less a GPS.
Endangered Silence causes me distress.

13. What is the best way to described the poet's attitude toward
    technology in general?
    (A) He hates it but also feels drawn to it.
    (B) He feels it is stalking him wherever he goes.
    (C) He does not like it, especially what it sounds like.
    (D) He knows more about it than he feels is healthy.
    (E) He senses that it is controlling people and possibly himself.

14. Based on the entirety of the poem, what do you think the poet
    implies the "silence" in line 4 is?
    (A) Delightful and exciting.
    (B) Sad and unsatisfying.
    (C) Harmonious yet terrifying.
    (D) Comforting and holy.
    (E) Tranquil and rare.

15. What is the rhetorical purpose of "laptops, iPads, cellphones" in line 2?
    (A) To provide examples of "all angles" in line 2.
    (B) To provide context for "radio and television" in line 1.
    (C) To provide sound-making devices that may be reduced in audio volume.
    (D) To provide ways to visit Venice through images and words.
    (E) To provide contrast to ancient communication methods.

16. What change in the poem occurs in Line 9?
    (A) The poem shifts from being about noise to being about a night out.
    (B) The silence is broken by noise.
    (C) The actions of the narrator become explicit.
    (D) The fist person perspective is introduced.
    (E) The problems of ancient transportation methods begin to be described.

17. Why does the poet likely feel "distress" in the last line?
    (A) He is worried about the effects of increasing technology on the world today.
    (B) He foresees that no one will be able to find quiet space in the future.
    (C) He correlates silence with endangered animals and is anxious about the destruction of both.
    (D) He misses his childhood and cannot go back to it.
    (E) He feels that conventional ideas about noise and silence are improving too slowly.

The Merchant of Venice

Act II, Scene V

by William Shakespeare (1564-1616)

In this excerpt, the servant Launcelot has just told his former employer, the Jewish merchant Shylock, that he will now instead serve the Christian merchant Bassanio. Launcelot brings both news about Shylock's planned visit to Bassanio and a secret message for Shylock's daughter, Jessica.

Scene: In front of Shylock's house. Shylock and Launcelot enter and Shylock calls out to Jessica repeatedly.

SHYLOCK

Well, thou shalt see, thy eyes shall be thy judge,
The difference of old Shylock and Bassanio: —
What, Jessica! — thou shalt not gormandise,
Lines As thou hast done with me: — What, Jessica! —
5   And sleep and snore, and rend apparel out; —
Why, Jessica, I say!

LAUNCELOT

Why, Jessica!

SHYLOCK

Who bids thee call? I do not bid thee call.

LAUNCELOT

Your worship was wont to tell me that
10 I could do nothing without bidding.

Enter Jessica

JESSICA

Call you? what is your will?

SHYLOCK

I am bid forth to supper, Jessica:
There are my keys. But wherefore should I go?
I am not bid for love; they flatter me:
15 But yet I'll go in hate, to feed upon
The prodigal Christian. Jessica, my girl,
Look to my house. I am right loath to go:
There is some ill a-brewing towards my rest,
For I did dream of money-bags to-night.

LAUNCELOT

20 I beseech you, sir, go: my young master
doth expect your reproach.

SHYLOCK

So do I his.

LAUNCELOT

And they have conspired together. I will not say you
shall see a masque; but if you do, then it was not
25 for nothing that my nose fell a-bleeding on
Black-Monday last at six o'clock i' the morning,
falling out that year on Ash-Wednesday was four
year, in the afternoon.

SHYLOCK

What, are there masques? Hear you me, Jessica:
30 Lock up my doors; and when you hear the drum
And the vile squealing of the wry-neck'd fife,
Clamber not you up to the casements then,
Nor thrust your head into the public street
To gaze on Christian fools with varnish'd faces,
35 But stop my house's ears, I mean my casements:
Let not the sound of shallow foppery enter
My sober house. By Jacob's staff, I swear,
I have no mind of feasting forth to-night:
But I will go. Go you before me, sirrah;
40 Say I will come.

LAUNCELOT

I will go before, sir. Mistress,
look out at window, for all this,
There will come a Christian by,
will be worth a Jewess' eye.

Launcelot exits

SHYLOCK

45   What says that fool of Hagar's offspring, ha?

JESSICA

His words were 'Farewell mistress;' nothing else.

SHYLOCK

The patch is kind enough, but a huge feeder;
Snail-slow in profit, and he sleeps by day
More than the wild-cat: drones hive not with me;
50   Therefore I part with him, and part with him
To one that would have him help to waste
His borrow'd purse. Well, Jessica, go in;
Perhaps I will return immediately:
Do as I bid you; shut doors after you:
55   Fast bind, fast find;
A proverb never stale in thrifty mind.

Shylock exits

JESSICA

Farewell; and if my fortune be not crost,
I have a father, you a daughter, lost.

Jessica exits

18. In line 17, when Shylock uses the word "loath," what does he most likely mean?
    (A) Hateful.
    (B) Reluctant.
    (C) Pleased.
    (D) Desirous.
    (E) Unlikely.

19. What literary technique is employed in Launcelot's statement, "my young master doth expect your reproach" (lines 20–21)?
    (A) Prestidigitation.
    (B) Malapropism.
    (C) Hermeneutics.
    (D) Spoonerism.
    (E) Invective.

20. Based on the context, what is the most likely definition of "casements" (lines 32 and 35)?
    (A) Instruments.
    (B) Ladders.
    (C) Masques.
    (D) Windows.
    (E) Doors.

21. All the following literary devices are used in lines 36–38 EXCEPT which one?
    (A) Personification.
    (B) Antithesis.
    (C) Alliteration.
    (D) Allusion.
    (E) Epistrophe.

22. What does Shylock mean when he says "and part with him / To one that would have him help to waste / His borrow'd purse" (lines 50–52)?
    (A) Launcelot's new employer is as wasteful and poor as he.
    (B) Launcelot will waste the money he borrowed.
    (C) Launcelot's new master likes to cross-dress.
    (D) Launcelot's new employer is a rich and wasteful libertine.
    (E) Shylock is deliberately being evasive.

23. Shylock compares Launcelot to all of the following in lines 47–56 EXCEPT what?
    (A) A fool.
    (B) A snail.
    (C) A feline.
    (D) A bee.
    (E) A proverb.

24. Which of the following is NOT a function of the selection?
    (A) To depict Shylock as a stereotypical Jew.
    (B) To give viewers reason to sympathize with Shylock.
    (C) To criticize Elizabethan music conventions.
    (D) To provide comic relief.
    (E) To develop the plot.

25. What does Jessica do in the passage?
    (A) Plans to attend the masque.
    (B) Secretly expresses her love for Launcelot.
    (C) Convinces Shylock to show mercy.
    (D) Lies to Shylock.
    (E) Reveals she stole money from Bassanio.

1.	B	11.	A	21.	E
2.	E	12.	D	22.	A
3.	C	13.	C	23.	E
4.	A	14.	E	24.	C
5.	A	15.	A	25.	D
6.	D	16.	C		
7.	D	17.	A		
8.	D	18.	B		
9.	C	19.	B		
10.	B	20.	D		

2. HOW TO WRITE IT

2.1 Writing a Sonnet: Easy to Difficult

by Evan Mantyk

WE START WITH the sonnet: the jewel in the crown of English poetry. Depending on your beginning skill or education, you can choose a level that is appropriate: challenging but still doable.

Put simply, a sonnet is a 14-line poem that originated in 13th-century Sicily. I'll take you through a simple guide that can lead to a basic sonnet in 10 minutes at the easy level to one that demonstrates literary mastery at the difficult level.

Level 1—Easy: A Sonnet in 10 Minutes

Poetry, at its best, is about those great, lofty, and universal themes like beauty, the meaning of life, and compassion for our fellow human beings. But it can also be humorous, unimportant, and topical. The genius of poetry is partially in the ability to convey a lot in a few words and make those few words catchy and attractive to your audience. To write a quick sonnet, we need something specific to focus on: a person, a painting, a book, a character, an event, a place, a relationship between two things, and so on. Can't find a topic? Just look for a picture or poster you like. Here is one of my favorite paintings:

"Sunrise on the Bay of Fundy" by William Bradford (1823–1892)

Now, whatever your topic is, imagine it is real. You are in front of it or in it. What are you feeling? Use your five senses and a sprinkle of imagination. Compare what you are thinking of to something ("the water was clear like crystal," "the water was crystal," or better yet "the crystalline water"). You can also repeat words and phrases for emphasis (*"What a* beautiful morning... *What a* gorgeous sea...").

Let the writing begin. Try to limit yourself to lines that are not more than 13 or 14 words long, and try to mostly end your sentences or thoughts where a line ends. It doesn't have to be one line per thought; you could have a thought that is four lines, for example, but try to wrap it up by the end of that fourth line, not in the middle of it. Capitalization of the first letter of each line and standard punctuation are optional.

Here we go:

On William Bradford's
"Sunrise on the Bay of Fundy"

The waves are bumpy and the wind blows hard,
But the sunrise is so beautiful to look at,
I could sit and look at it forever;
I feel like a new day is beginning and everything is going
To be okay, especially because there is
This guy there for me to talk to.
Why do people, like me, like to look at the water so much;
Why not just look at the land all the time?
There is something special about the water.
Maybe it's the clear horizon line, like a desert.
It makes you feel big and opened up to the sky.
Openness makes you feel cleansed,
Pure, like the garbage can has been emptied,
And powerful, like you could go anywhere.

Done! You have written a sonnet in free verse (without any rhyme or meter). Check the timer.

Level 2—Medium: Rhyme-y Poetry

Many people will say that poetry isn't poetry if it doesn't rhyme. Traditionally speaking, this is generally true of short poems like sonnets. The word "sonnet," after all, means "little song" in Italian, and song lyrics, you might have noticed, usually rhyme.

If you aren't naturally good at rhyming, there are plenty of sources for rhyme words at your local library or online. There are entire rhyming dictionaries. If you can't find a rhyme for your word, the tactic is usually to swap your original word with a different one that has the same meaning. For this, I recommend a thesaurus, similarly found at your local library or online. Or, even rewrite the first line and first rhyme entirely in order to achieve the second line and/or rhyme you want. You can also rearrange the order of the verb, noun, and various phrases of a sentence. The rhyming poet must be flexible and agile.

Partial rhymes can also work. For example, the notoriously difficult-to-rhyme word "orange" can be half rhymed with forage, storage, grange, strange, angel, and so on. You can also use alliterative rhymes that focus on the beginning of the word. For orange, you might use oratory, orangutan, ordinary, Orion. Here's an orange poem quickly composed for you:

The Orange Poem

I listened to the oratory
On the topic of the color orange;
At first I thought it ordinary,
Someone said "red and yellow make orange,"
But then it got a bit more strange:
He said, "A one-hundred-color range
Forms the continuum of orange."

Ready to rhyme? Next step is your rhyme scheme. If you are a beginner, it is easiest to just rhyme the lines as you go. In fact, many great poets, such Geoffrey Chaucer, used this technique. Lines 1 and 2 end with the first rhyming pair (or couplet); lines 3 and 4 form the next rhyming pair, and so on. If you continue this way to the end, the rhyme scheme of your sonnet is expressed this way:

aa bb cc dd ee ff gg

To make it clearer, here is a quickly composed poem with an aabba rhyme scheme:

I saw a great big dog (a)
Standing on top of a log (a)
I ran away (b)
But then it came my way (b)
And said, "May I join your jog?" (a)

The rhyme scheme used by William Shakespeare in the early 1600s was a bit more complicated. This is the typical rhyme scheme for a Shakespearean sonnet:

abab cdcd efef gg

Another classic and more difficult sonnet rhyme scheme is that used by the Italian poet Petrarch in the 1300s:

abbaabba cdcdcd *or* abbaabba cdecde

Now, let's return to the first two lines of our example poem on William Bradford's painting. These are the first two lines currently:

> The waves are bumpy and the wind blows hard
> But the sunrise is so beautiful to look at

We'll try for the easiest type of rhyming, in which each line rhymes with the next one. After a little shifting and head scratching, we get this:

> The waves are bumpy and the hard wind blows
> But the beauty of the sunrise shows

Continue doing this for each line and you have a rhyming sonnet that looks more traditional than a free-verse sonnet. The problem with the free-verse sonnet is that people may not see any difference between your poem and ordinary writing, or prose. Rhyming solves this problem quite well.

Level 3—Medium-Difficult: Poetry with Rhyme and Structure

If you want to produce a sonnet with greater elegance and discipline that connects more fully with thousands of years of great poets, then you should consider a stronger structure. Traditional or classical poets usually adhere to more rigid structure than is found in the easy-level, free-verse poem. In classical Chinese poetry, for example, each line has the same number of characters. In classical French poetry, poets often count the syllables. The classical Greek and English poets depend on the number and placement of stresses. In most classical cultures, these structures create a kind of universal order and intricate beauty, so that any missing word or stress upsets the entire order. It is as the Renaissance architect Leon Battista Alberti said, "Beauty is that reasoned harmony of all the parts within a body, so that nothing may be added, taken away, or altered, but for the worse."

Additionally, the sonnet itself matches other sonnets, not only in the number of lines but also the inner structure that has been used in sonnets for hundreds of years. Using a classical model leaves a well-structured poem resonating both backward and forward in history in ways that a free-verse sonnet cannot. This is magnificent! Yet, also difficult.

For English poetry, the easiest way to provide some clear structure is by counting syllables, creating what is known as syllabic verse. Not sure how many syllables a word has? Use a dictionary to see clearly how many syllables a word has. You can also remove syllables—change "mirror" to "mirr'r," for example—or add syllables that people don't normally pronounce, such as "poém" (pronounced "poh-EM"). Sonnets usually have 10 syllables per line (with meter, which we'll discuss later, this is called iambic pentameter).

Here we go. Our original free-verse sonnet is revised to include a Shakespearean sonnet rhyme scheme and 10 syllables per line. (Capitalization of the first letter of each line and standard punctuation should be included for this level. Indentation is optional and purely a matter of personal style):

On William Bradford's
"Sunrise on the Bay of Fundy"

Steady currents of wind blow 'cross my face,
Steady currents of water rock my feet,
As the sun rises in its brilliant grace,
The raucous world seems so smooth and so sweet.
Our small vessel has not yet raised its sail,
My shipmate and I contemplate the day,
And what our minor journey will entail,
Nothing so important to again say.
And yet the immensity of the dawn,
Accentuated by vast horizon,
Is like a giant knot that's been undone,
And releases each trespass and treason.
    Larger and better ships may sail around,
    Yet the expanse of my heart knows no bound.

Level 4—Difficult: Sonnet in Iambic Pentameter and Careful Attention to Meaning

More difficult and rewarding than counting syllables is looking at the meter. This is real, adult English poetry. The meter is the use of hard stresses and soft stresses to create structure. The iamb is the most standard and natural unit in the English language. It is made up of a hard stress followed by a soft stress. Iambic pentameter is the traditional meter for a sonnet, and it is the most common in classical English poetry in general. You can feel the rhythm of a poem more clearly when it's composed with meter rather than with syllable counting. For iambic pentameter, the rhythm should feel something like "dee–DUM, dee–DUM, dee–DUM, dee–DUM, dee–DUM." Here are some examples:

> One iamb: I ***am***
> Four iambs: I ***am*** a ***man*** and ***noth***ing ***more***.
> Five iambs (iambic pentameter): I ***am*** a ***man*** who ***tries*** and ***noth***ing ***more***

For reference, the opposite of an iamb is the trochee, which is a hard stress followed by a soft stress:

> One trochee: ***Noth***ing
> Four trochees: ***Noth***ing ***good*** can ***come*** from ***ly***ing

Note that a hard or soft stress sometimes does not correspond to a single syllable and this is perfectly normal. For example, you could write: "I ***am*** a ***cap***tain and ***noth***ing ***more***." There are two syllables after "***cap***" that form the soft stress and this is still considered a line of four iambs (or iambic tetrameter). Thus, a real line of iambic pentameter (such as the eleven syllables in "To ***be*** or ***not*** to ***be***: that ***is*** the ***quest***ion") will often not have exactly ten syllables. Of course if you use too many deviations then you risk losing the rhythm of the meter.

Also important is the meaning behind the words. The sonnet is generally broken up into the first eight lines (the octave) and then the following six lines (the sestet), with the turn (or volta) in between. The octave sets up an idea, establishing it fully, and then something changes or something different happens with that idea in those last six lines. It is a small journey. Particularly if we look at the

Shakespearean sonnet, the sestet could be further broken up into four lines (quatrain) and a concluding two lines (couplet). In this pattern, our 14-line sonnet has three distinct sections, going from eight lines to four lines to two lines. Each section is divided by a factor of two, and the second and third sections act to continuously distill the idea of the poet down to its very essence. From this perspective, every single word and phrase needs to be carefully thought over and chosen. Here, there can be no filler words or "yeah, I just put that there because it rhymes." Every letter and comma needs to be working toward the idea and painting it with the clearest colors and most accurate perspective and proportion. Here is our highest and final incarnation of our sonnet:

On William Bradford's "Sunrise on the Bay of Fundy"

A firm wind slaps me on my boat and face,
Waves rolling try to knock me off my feet,
And yet the world is lit with rising grace,
Which makes my roughshod life seem soft and sweet.
Our ship has not yet raised its measly sail,
My mate and I have much hard work ahead,
And yet, how calmly forward blows the gale
That lifts my soul to where the angels tread,
To where our hearts and minds are freed and cleansed,
Expanded by the wide horizon line,
To where the softest clouds above ascend
Into a color free from Earth's confines,
    Beyond the mighty ships that gather round,
    Beyond my flesh, which to the sea is bound.

Here are the first four lines with the hard stresses in the iambic pentameter highlighted:

a *firm* wind *slaps* me *on* my *boat* and *face*,
Waves *roll*ing *try* to *tip* me *off* my *feet*,
And *yet* the *world* is *lit* with *ris*ing *grace*,
Which *makes* my *rough*shod *life* seem *soft* and *sweet*.

2.2 How to Write a Haiku

by G.M.H. Thompson

THE JAPANESE-INSPIRED haiku is perhaps the most well-known and often used form of poetry today. Schoolchildren the English-speaking world over know that a haiku is five syllables in the first line followed by seven syllables in the second line followed by a final five syllables in the third line. It's as simple as counting, right? Well, if that was right, this essay would end right here.

For, although the haiku is perhaps the most well-known form of poetry, it is also probably the least well-understood. The contents of a legitimate and interesting haiku must do about five different things all at once in a very tight space.

Perhaps it will be easiest to start out with what a haiku is not. Many haiku poets concentrate solely on the 5-7-5 syllable count and the fact that what they are writing is a haiku, every so often chucking in superficial Japan-esque imagery, such as lanterns, cherry blossoms, willow trees, Mt. Fuji, or anything out of *Cowboy Bebop* or Miyazaki (and that's if you're lucky—if you're unlucky, it's from *Dragon Ball Z*, *Full Metal Alchemist*, or *Yu-Gi-Oh!*). This leads to glib, epigrammatic, syllabic poems that go something like this:

A Bad Haiku

Archipelago:
There are perhaps a million
Haiku with that word

What makes a good haiku? Fundamentally, the art of haiku is the art of saying by not saying but by suggesting allusively.

1. Firstly, the haiku is a **statement on humanity's relationship with nature**. The master haiku poet Basho (1644–1694) wrote this often repeated haiku:

At the ancient pond,
A frog leaps and plunges in
The sound of water

—Basho

Here the poem is ostensibly about a frog, but this all changes with "the sound of water" since it is something perceived presumably by the poet. Thus, the connection or relationship may be very subtle. Here is a haiku I wrote:

Harem

Water lilies bloom
Beside a crystal fountain
In the Sultan's court

If the poem were about lilies alone, it would not be a haiku. The relationship comes alive through the Sultan, although he may not necessarily be there, and the fact that this is a harem and the lilies may not be lilies at all but beautiful women devoted to the Sultan.

2. The second vital element of a haiku is that it be **in the present**, which is to say, each haiku is focused on a moment and the moment is like a very short film. This can at times be hard to convey or pick up on as a reader, but it helps to write in the present tense exclusively and to focus on action with things doing things. Using gerunds (-ing words) is also pretty handy for grounding the poem in the present. For instance, this Basho poem would clearly be less effective if the last line said "flew in the darkness":

A flash of lightning
The screech of a night heron
Flying in darkness

—Basho

In a single moment, the lightning's menace is elegantly complement-ed by the night heron's plight in the dark storm to create a mood of lost hopelessness, perhaps reflecting the poet's psychological state at the precise moment of the haiku's composition, which appears to be quite desperate.

3. The third key thing a haiku must do is **twist in the third line**: Traditional Japanese poetry does this through the use of a "cutting word." Unfortunately, there is no real equivalent for that in the way the English language works. The closest parallel to this twist in other forms of English poetics is the final two lines of a Shakespearean sonnet, or the final couplet of an Elizabethan soliloquy. The haiku cut creates a curious and very non-Western disruption, or twist, to the flow of idea developed so far in the poem, yet one that forms a new flow of the idea. Observe the following Basho haiku, his death poem:

> Sick on my journey
> Only my dreams will wander
> The desolate moors
> —Basho

Here, we do not know if it is the traveler on the desolate moors or the dreams somehow on them, or both on them. The third line disrupts the traditional Western disconnection between mind and matter. This is my haiku:

Honey Bee

> ebony and gold
> newsprung flowers kissed to life:
> the earth reborn sweet

In the final line, we see that the earth is in fact alive and the perspective has gone from tiny, to normal, to large beyond our view.

4. The fourth tenet of haiku is image. Specifically, **two images**. That is the ideal number of images a haiku should have: With only one image, there is little room for action and little room for change; with more than two images, things often get said that don't need to be said and the haiku quickly becomes slack and lost within itself. Juxtaposing two images with a colon, dash, or comma, without doing anything else, can be enough to make a great haiku. See this example by haiku master Yosa Buson (1716–1783):

A pear flower blooms,
A woman reads a letter—
Beneath the moon's light
        —Buson

The tight juxtaposition of the images of the pear flower blossoming and the woman reading a (probably amorous) letter beneath the moonlight suggests that there is some deep, mysterious, almost mythical connection between them.

5. The fifth element of a traditional, proper haiku is the **seasonal word**. This can be as obvious as "spring," "autumnal," or "March," but it can also be a lot more subtle and interesting. For instance, mentioning plum blossoms is a reference to very early spring or very late winter (depending on where one is in Japan). Mentioning the cuckoo's song alludes to summer and also to death, as another baby bird has to die for a cuckoo to survive and thus sing. The cicada also refers to summer. There are many other veiled seasonal references like that, many of which I do not actually have knowledge of, but nonetheless, here is an example of a Buson haiku with a seasonal word:

The white plum blossoms
Almost through yesterday's night
A new day coming
        —Buson

Here, the white plum blossoms refer to early spring/late winter, and the poem itself is about the changing of one year into the next, with the image of yesterday's residual darkness turning into the new day's nascent light serving as a metaphor for this transformation. On a deeper and more important level, this poem is about passing from the world of the living, "yesterday's night," into some world beyond, "a new day coming," as it is Buson's death poem, that is, his last poem before he died.

Rhyming?

Regarding rhyming, traditional Japanese haiku is unrhymed because every Japanese word ends in a vowel sound, so there are really only about six rhymes in the entire language, effectively ruling rhyming right out as being almost comically simple and stupid (the opposite of English's rhyming troubles, funnily). That being said, there is no real reason why haiku should not rhyme in English. Here is my rhymed haiku:

Antioch

who knows and who cares
and who goes where roses wear
the pale face of death

Here, the rhyme serves to link the first two lines, and the third line is nicely set apart from them by its lack of rhyme, this absence in and of itself serving as the haiku's twist or "cutting word." If all three lines rhymed (a tempting choice, admittedly, but one that is best avoided), this haiku would not succeed in what little way it does.

A Final Note Regarding Inspiration

To obtain the tangible inspiration necessary to actually sit down and write a haiku, it is best to focus on specific moments of nature observed personally by the haiku poet, and to think about how these instances were moments of transformation or change or revelation. For while haiku can be constructed using the imagination, it is far easier to rely upon lived experience. Let reality and memory do the work, and don't feel beat up if it's difficult to dream up great haiku using pure imagination (it is tremendously difficult to do that). Go to a park, or to the zoo, or to a nature preserve, or to a forest, or to a jungle, or to an aquarium, and notice. Notice and notice more wherever you go and wherever you are and whatever you are doing, for it is observation above all else that will lead to writing good haiku. And notice the little things, for those are the things that no one seems to notice, and noticing those little things often makes for the best haiku.

The History of Haiku

The composition of poetry in Japan using lines that are five and seven syllables in length has occurred since at least the 8th century, and probably long before that; that date simply being the century in which the first book of Japanese poems was composed. From at least this time, such poetry was pursued by members of every island in the archipelago of Japan, no matter how low or high, although the considerably greater amount of free time and education the nobility possessed has always led to an over-representation of their social order within the ocean that is Japanese verse. Note that although Japanese does not technically have "syllables" like English does, it can be said to have de facto syllables, provided, of course, that one is not a slave to pedantry.

One of these forms was the tanka, a form that can be thought of as a tercet (three lines) of 5-7-5 syllables followed by what can be thought of as a couplet (two lines) of 7-7 syllables. (Traditional Japanese poetry does not use line breaks as a strong, active element of poetic structure as traditional European poetry does, but it is best to think of things as they have been stated outside these parentheses.) Additionally, Japanese is not a language of stresses as is English or German, nor does it have any equivalents thereof such as the longs and shorts of Latin and Greek. Every syllable is given nearly equal weight when pronounced in Japanese, like in French, so traditional Japanese poetry is strictly—and it really is very strict on this sole metrical point—syllabic.

Another of these 5-7 forms was what would come to be called renga, which is best to think of as a series of tanka stacked on top of one another. Note that the plural of renga is renga, the plural of tanka is tanka, the plural of haiku is haiku, and so forth.

Formally, renga go 5-7-5 7-7 5-7-5 7-7 5-7-5 7-7 ... , ending on a couplet traditionally. The renga is a collaborative poem that by the 17th century had established itself as the dominant long-form of poetic expression in the Japanese literary tradition. One poet would begin a renga with a hokku, which is a tercet of five syllables followed by seven syllables followed by five syllables (coincidence—I think not!). Another poet would add to this a couplet of seven syllables followed by seven syllables. Then, a third poet would add a tercet structurally identical to the first stanza (that is, 5-7-5), but the key here was that the poem formed by the hokku and the couplet alone had to be different in content and character than the poem formed by the couplet and the third stanza when looked at alone. In other words, the third stanza introduced a curious and very non-Western disruption, or twist, to the flow of idea developed so far in the poem, yet one that formed a new flow of the idea with the second stanza when considered without the first hokku. A couplet structurally identical to the second stanza was then added, often by yet another poet, and like the third stanza, this fourth stanza had to disrupt the flow of idea by forming a new flow of idea with the third stanza that was different than the flow of idea between the third and second stanzas, or the flow of idea between the second and first stanzas.

This process often went on for exactly 36 stanzas (forming a kasan), and there were many rules as to the content that the participants were to write. The themes were almost invariably humanity's relationship with nature or humanity's relationship with humanity—the same two themes of traditional haiku—and similarly, seasonal imagery was employed heavily.

Yet, by far the most vital element of the renga was the hokku, the opening tercet of 5-7-5, as this set the overall tone and mood of the entire series. Owing to this special status, poets would study and practice the construction of hokku with especial fervor and concentration. Groups of hokku began, by the mid-17th century, to be collected and displayed independent of the renga that spawned them, and the acclaimed Japanese poet Basho interspersed hokku in his prose travel journals, inventing a new form of prose-poetry: the haibun. Later, as you might have guessed, the hokku was renamed haiku. Thus concludes a not so short synopsis of the history of haiku.

2.3 The Mechanics of Classical Poetry

by Dusty Grein

I AM GOING to lay out the basics of writing classical-style poetry in English, based on standard poetry terms and references. This discussion will focus on classical poetry, that is, rhyming, metered poems.

Please keep in mind that the natural flow of poetic pronunciation and patterns will be influenced by your diction, and sometimes even your accent. This exploration will be done using the diction that comes naturally to me. I am from the Pacific Northwest in the United States, and I speak with no dialect or discernible accent (at least not to me).

Terms

In order to build a poem, and to be able to discuss, explain, and look at samples of poems, we must define some terms. Some of this may sound simplistic, but there are those who struggle with the concepts, so I would like to begin with some very rudimentary basics concerning words, sounds, and cadence.

Syllables (Word Building Blocks)

Syllables are single sounds, and the English language is composed of words built using these sounds. Some words, "cone" for example, contain only one syllable (sound burst). Other words, such as "circle" (cir-cle), contain two syllables. We have words built from any number of syllables—for example, "constitutional" has five syllables (con-sti-tu-tion-al).

Stress (Emphasis)

Syllables are the building blocks of sound that we use to build words, but we don't usually talk in monotone (unless you are attempting to do an impression of a robot). Instead, we vary the pitch, volume, and strength of our pronunciation of the syllables in our words. This is the stress, which can be soft (unstressed) or hard (stressed). The word "circle," for instance, has a stressed syllable followed by an unstressed syllable. It is usually pronounced "CIR-cle."

Sometimes our meaning may be completely different, depending on how we pronounce a single word. For example, if someone says, "How are you *today*?" we can immediately get the sense that something significant happened earlier, probably yesterday. Although more subtle than the use of italics, classical poetry is built using emphasized or stressed syllables in patterns that allow the words to be read with a noticeable, almost melodic, cadence and flow.

Poetic Feet

This is one of the hardest parts of poetic patterns to grasp, but if you stay with me, and try my tapping methods, you can learn exactly what these words mean, and how we use them to understand and build poems.

Classical poetry in English is usually composed using pairs and trios of stressed and unstressed syllables, in metered rhyming patterns. These syllable pairs and trios are known as poetic feet. Each foot contains a combination of hard (stressed) and soft (unstressed) syllables. In English poetry, there are five basic poetic feet used. Here they are, with their syllable counts and patterns. In these examples, the hard syllables are in all capital letters.

> **iamb** — 2-syllable foot: A soft syllable followed by a stressed one, as in the word "adjust" (ah–JUST). Used to create iambic lines.

> **trochee** — 2-syllable foot: A hard syllable followed by a soft one, as in the word "shatter" (SHAT–ter). Used to create trochaic lines.

spondee — 2-syllable foot: Two equally stressed syllables, as in the word "breakdown" (BRAKE-DOWN). Used to create spondaic lines.

dactyl — 3-syllable foot: A hard syllable followed by two soft ones, as in "carefully" (KAYR-ful-ly). Used to create dactylic lines.

anapest — 3-syllable foot: Two softs syllables followed by a hard one, as in "comprehend" (kom-pre-HEND). Used to create anapestic lines.

The above rely on the way that the words are commonly pronounced. One could still potentially pronounce "breakdown" as "brake-DOWN" or "BRAKE-down" in a poem, but the more such deviations from the normal pronunciation are used, the greater the likelihood that the rhythm of the poem will be weakened or lost for the reader.

There are other patterns of poetic feet, but they are very rarely used in classical English poetry. Here is a complete list of two- and three-syllable feet, with a syllable count and pattern, using "DUM" for the hard syllables and "dee" for the soft ones. By tapping your finger hard on the "DUM" and soft on the "dee," you will get an idea of the sound stress patterns that can be created.

<u>Syllable Count: Foot Name: Pattern</u>

2 syllables: pyrrhus: dee-dee
2 syllables: iamb: dee-DUM
2 syllables: trochee: DUM-dee
2 syllables: spondee: DUM-DUM
3 syllables: tribrach: dee-dee-dee
3 syllables: dactyl: DUM-dee-dee
3 syllables: amphibrach: dee-DUM-dee
3 syllables: anapest: dee-dee-DUM
3 syllables: bacchius: dee-DUM-DUM
3 syllables: antibacchius: DUM-DUM-dee
3 syllables: cretic: DUM-dee-DUM
3 syllables: molossus: DUM-DUM-DUM

Line Meter

Poetic meter is a count of the number of feet in a line. Most poems are written with between one and eight poetic feet per line. This creates the following poetic metric line types, based on how many feet are in the line:

<u>Number of Feet: Meter Name</u>

1 foot: monometer
2 feet: dimeter
3 feet: trimeter
4 feet: tetrameter
5 feet: pentameter
6 feet: hexameter
7 feet: heptameter
8 feet: octameter

Perhaps the most famous type of line is that used by Shakespeare in many of his works, both prosaic and poetic—iambic pentameter, or five pairs of iambs, for a total of about 10 syllables.

Often, poets will use a line with a missing first or last syllable, for emphasis and strength in their patterns. These lines are referred to as catalectic or headless.

Rhyme Pattern / Stanzas

The final ingredient in the creation of the classic rhyming poem is the number and pattern of rhyming lines. The final syllable or syllables in the metered lines are set to rhyme with each other in many different patterns, and the number of these lines determines the stanza length.

Stanzas are generally sets of lines that are separated by a blank line. The most common are stanzas containing four lines, also known as a quatrain, but there are many varied types of stanzas, from the simple two-line couplet to complex forms like the sonnet or sestina.

<u>Line Length: Stanza Type Name</u>

2 lines: couplet
3 lines: triplet

4 lines: quatrain
5 lines: quintrain, quintet
6 lines: sestet
7 lines: septet
8 lines: octet, octave

In order to show the rhyming pattern in poetic stanzas, I will use the labeling method of describing the rhyming lines using letters so that all lines identified with the same letter rhyme with each other.

Examples

Now that we have a vocabulary, we can examine poetry with a common language. Probably the most common form of poetry, which we learn when we are very young, is the quatrain in an A B C B pattern. These poems may consist of different meters and feet counts, even having them mixed, as long as the second and fourth lines rhyme:

> (A) I loved you before,
> (B) I love you still,
> (C) I always have and
> (B) I always will.

This is a simplistic form of poetry and is not truly metered. It is still a valuable form of poetry, and the greeting card industry would be lost without it. For our purposes of exploration, however, we will leave this simplistic approach behind and look at more organized and structured poems. Note that in the following samples, the hard syllables are bold, italicized, and underlined.

One of the simplest structured poems ever written is a couplet of two rhyming lines titled "Fleas," written in trochaic monometer (a single trochee per line):

Fleas

> (A) ***<u>Ad</u>***am
> (A) ***<u>had</u>*** 'em.

Another very popular poem, "A Visit From St. Nicholas," was written in anapestic tetrameter quatrains (four anapests per line, four lines per stanza) with an A A B B pattern, with the B lines missing the first syllable (catalectic):

> (A) 'Twas the **_night_** before **_Christ_**mas and **_all_** through the **_house_**
> (A) Not a **_crea_**ture was **_stir_**ring, not **_ev_**en a **_mouse_**.
> (B) The **_stock_**ings were **_hung_** by the **_chim_**ney with **_care_**
> (B) In **_hopes_** that Saint **_Nich_**olas **_soon_** would be **_there_**.

The last example we'll look at for now are lines from Shakespeare's *A Midsummer Night's Dream*. This fantastical play was written in iambic pentameter quatrains (four-line stanzas, with five iambs per line) in A A B B pattern:

> (A) And **_I_** do **_love_** thee: **_there_**fore, **_go_** with **_me_**;
> (A) I'll **_give_** thee **_fair_**ies **_to_** at**_tend_** on **_thee_**,
> (B) And **_they_** shall **_fetch_** thee **_jew_**els **_from_** the **_deep_**,
> (B) And **_sing_** while **_thou_** on **_pressed_** flow**_ers_** dost **_sleep_**;

So now we have a basic grasp on classical poetry terms and forms. In reading classical poems from now, you can examine their rhyming patterns and meters, a process known as scansion.

2.4 How to Write a Villanelle

by Dusty Grein

HAILING FROM 15TH- and 16th-century French and Italian roots, the villanelle is arguably one of the strongest repeating refrain forms in classical poetry.

Its use of two alternating refrains creates an echo that reverberates throughout its mere 19 lines. The result is an intensity that can be both haunting and powerful. It is this intensity that leads the villanelle to most often be used in the dramatic creation of strong emotions, or deeply emotional themes.

It is a very rigidly structured form, but due to its limited rhyming foot scheme—only two rhyme sounds are used—and its use of two refrain lines, it can be less difficult to compose than many other structured forms. The poem is composed of six stanzas: five tercets followed by a single quatrain, each of which uses at least one of the refrain lines, in alternating sequence.

Here is the basic pattern, using A1 for the first refrain, A2 for the second, and (a) and (b) for the other lines. Note that all of the lowercase and uppercase letter A's rhyme with each other. Each stanza is shown on a single line here, but is made of individual lines in the poem:

Stanza 1: A1, b, A2
Stanza 2: a, b, A1
Stanza 3: a, b, A2
Stanza 4: a, b, A1
Stanza 5: a, b, A2
Stanza 6: a, b, A1, A2.

Meter

Technically the villanelle doesn't require a meter, but the majority of classical poets have used solid meters when crafting them; this helps to create the rhythmic cadence that is part of the form's magic.

Perhaps the most famous villanelle ever written is "Do Not Go Gentle Into That Good Night" by Dylan Thomas. Written in iambic pentameter, it is a remarkable 19 lines:

Do Not Go Gentle Into That Good Night

By Dylan Thomas (1914–1953)

Do not go gentle into that good night,
Old age should burn and rave at close of day;
Rage, rage against the dying of the light.

Though wise men at their end know dark is right,
Because their words had forked no lightning they
Do not go gentle into that good night.

Good men, the last wave by, crying how bright
Their frail deeds might have danced in a green bay,
Rage, rage against the dying of the light.

Wild men who caught and sang the sun in flight,
And learn, too late, they grieved it on its way,
Do not go gentle into that good night.

Grave men, near death, who see with blinding sight
Blind eyes could blaze like meteors and be gay,
Rage, rage against the dying of the light.

And you, my father, there on the sad height,
Curse, bless, me now with your fierce tears, I pray.
Do not go gentle into that good night.
Rage, rage against the dying of the light.

Creating One of Your Own

Crafting a villanelle presents us with a couple challenges. The first, and most important, is to choose a meter and create your refrains. For this, you must use your own poetic judgment and creativity.

Keep in mind that these two lines will echo throughout the body of the poem. They must work together, in both your opening stanza as well as the final statement in the ending quatrain. These two lines must also stand alone, as the final line in each tercet stanza along the way.

I have found that choosing a theme makes it easier to build rhyming metered lines. For this example I have chosen to use friendship as a theme, and I am going to use iambic pentameter—not because it's required for the form, but because I like the cadence it produces. With this in mind, after some deliberation, my two refrain lines will be:

> (A1) Hold my hand in yours; we'll make it through.
> (A2) For no one understands me like you do.

This meter decision and the creation of these two lines is the most difficult part of the villanelle crafting process. Once you have written these echoing lines that fit together, you can create the framework of poetic feet that will constitute the poem itself. Following the villanelle's pattern, I get the structure below.

Note that in this pattern, (–) represents a soft syllable and (=)represents a hard one, with (|) as a separator between feet.

(A1) Hold my hand in yours; we'll make it through.
(b) – = | – = | – = | – = | – =
(A2) For no one understands me like you do.
(a) – = | – = | – = | – = | – =
(b) – = | – = | – = | – = | – =
(A1) Hold my hand in yours; we'll make it through.
(a) – = | – = | – = | – = | – =
(b) – = | – = | – = | – = | – =
(A2) For no one understands me like you do.
(a) – = | – = | – = | – = | – =
(b) – = | – = | – = | – = | – =
(A1) Hold my hand in yours; we'll make it through.
(a) – = | – = | – = | – = | – =
(b) – = | – = | – = | – = | – =
(A2) For no one understands me like you do.
(a) – = | – = | – = | – = | – =
(b) – = | – = | – = | – = | – =
(A1) Hold my hand in yours; we'll make it through.
(A2) For no one understands me like you do.

As you can see, we need five (a) lines and six (b) lines to complete the poem, and these must flow within the theme. Since I already know the rhyme sound for (a), I chose the following list: you, too, blue, new, view. I then chose six keywords that rhymed with each other and that felt like good accents to this list: comprehend, friend, pretend, send, mend, end. By plugging these into the pattern, and then creating iambic feet that rounded out the meter, I was able to build a nice poem that fit the theme.

Hold My Hand in Yours

by Dusty Grein

Hold my hand in yours; we'll make it through.
If life becomes too hard to comprehend,
for no one understands me like you do.

Along life's lonely road, I'll walk with you.
When times are hard, please know you have a friend.
Hold my hand in yours; we'll make it through.

I'm here for you. You give me your strength too;
my courage is no longer just pretend,
for no one understands me like you do.

My friend, I'll cheer you up when you are blue,
A smile, my heart to yours will always send.
Hold my hand in yours; we'll make it through.

If I am down, you make me feel brand new
You know the way, my broken heart to mend,
for no one understands me like you do.

Though oft times life presents a horrid view,
Together we can face the bitter end.
Hold my hand in yours; we'll make it through,
for no one understands me like you do.

It may not be Dylan Thomas, but I kind of like the result. It could stand a bit of editing and some polishing, but it is a solid foundation.

As you can see, the crafting of a classic metered poem, even in a form as rigid as the villanelle, is something that can be challenging yet fun. Writing metered rhymes in these types of forms will help you grow as a poet, and I encourage you to challenge yourself and see what happens.

2.5 How to Write a Rondeau

by E.V. Wyler

CREATED BY FRENCH troubadours during the Middle Ages, the rondeau is valued for its lovely lyrical qualities. The tone of a rondeau may be joyful, mournful, or anything in between. An example of a famous rondeau is "In Flanders Fields," which was composed by the Canadian soldier and physician John McCrae at the World War I battlefront on May 3, 1915, during the second battle of Ypres, Belgium:

In Flanders Fields

by John McCrae (1872–1918)

In Flanders fields the poppies blow
Between the crosses, row on row,
That mark our place; and in the sky
The larks, still bravely singing, fly
Scarce heard amid the guns below.

We are the Dead. Short days ago
We lived, felt dawn, saw sunset glow,
Loved and were loved, and now we lie
In Flanders fields.

Take up our quarrel with the foe:
To you from failing hands we throw
The torch; be yours to hold it high.
If ye break faith with us who die
We shall not sleep, though poppies grow
In Flanders fields.

As you can hear from reading John McCrae's poem aloud, the repetition of the phrase "In Flanders fields" emphasizes its meaning, creating a poignant echo effect as the poem unfolds. This repetition, along with the use of only two rhyming patterns, creates the poem's hypnotic enchantment.

Although several different formats of the rondeau have evolved, this tutorial pertains to the longer version with three stanzas: a (5-line) quintet, a (4-line) quatrain, and a (6-line) sestet.

Summary

15 lines: divided into 3 stanzas (5 lines, 4 lines, 6 lines)
8 syllables per line (except for the two 4-syllable refrains)
2 rhyming schemes (8 "A" end-rhymes and 5 "B" end-rhymes)
8 "A" rhymes + 5 "B" rhymes + 2 refrains = 15 lines
The first 4 syllables of Line 1 are the refrain (for Lines 9 and 15)

Visual Layout

Line 1: End-Rhyme "A" — 4-syllable opening phrase + 4 syllables = 8 syllables
Line 2: End-Rhyme "A" — 8 syllables
Line 3: End-Rhyme "B" — 8 syllables
Line 4: End-Rhyme "B" — 8 syllables
Line 5: End-Rhyme "A" — 8 syllables

Line 6: End-Rhyme "A" — 8 syllables
Line 7: End-Rhyme "A" — 8 syllables
Line 8: End-Rhyme "B" — 8 syllables
Line 9: Refrain (Line 1's 4-syllable opening phrase)

Line 10: End-Rhyme "A" — 8 syllables
Line 11: End-Rhyme "A" — 8 syllables
Line 12: End-Rhyme "B" — 8 syllables
Line 13: End-Rhyme "B" — 8 syllables
Line 14: End-Rhyme "A" — 8 syllables
Line 15: Refrain (Line 1's 4-syllable opening phrase)

One factor in deciding to compose a rondeau (as opposed to a villanelle, sonnet, and so on) is the selection of a strong mood-inducing refrain that works as an opening, a mid-poem repetition, and a closing. In the early stages of a composition, it is best to begin with a simple image or idea. Think of yourself as putting together the pieces of a puzzle whose picture can only be seen in your mind and felt in your heart. I'd compare the puzzle's straight-line perimeter pieces to the rondeau's skeletal structure. As the poet creates the rhyme, meter, and plot, the poem's stanzas continue forming, like the landscape of a scenic puzzle, until finally the last "piece" is placed, and the completed rondeau emerges from the cocoon of the poet's heart.

Lastly, here is an example of a rondeau written by a living classical poet:

My Mirror Grinned

by Sathya Narayana

My mirror grinned at my first gray.
With rearing youth, it's my first fray.
Disturbed, with care I plucked that bane,
next day to find one more, again!
I cried and sighed and went astray!

That's how began my darkest day
with whitest hair and day by day
at deepening my fear and pain ...
my mirror grinned!

With no concern at my dismay
went on my hair, to well betray
with more and more albescent strains;
until one day remarked Miss Jane,
I looked smarter with that new gray!
My mirror grinned!

2.6 How to Write a Triolet

by Carol Smallwood

THE TRIOLET IS a medieval French poetry form that has eight lines and was introduced to the English language by poets in the 17th century:

1. A
2. B
3. a Rhymes with 1st line.
4. A Identical to 1st line.
5. a Rhymes with 1st line.
6. b Rhymes with 2nd line.
7. A Identical to 1st line.
8. B Identical to 2nd line.

Note that lines 1, 4, and 7 are identical. Lines 2 and 8 are identical. Lines 3, 5, 6 are single, different. The rhyme scheme, ABaAabAB, may be in iambic tetrameter such as this spiritual triolet:

Triolet III

by Patrick Carey (1624–1657)

Yes, my dear Lord, I've found it so;
No joys but thine are purely sweet;
Other delights come mixt with woe,
Yes, my dear Lord, I've found it so.
Pleasure at courts is but in show,
With true content in cells we meet;
Yes, my dear Lord, I've found it so;
No joys but thine are purely sweet.

Other types of meter may also work, as seen in this translated classic French triolet:

Rondel

by Jean Froissart (1337–1404)

Love, love, what wilt thou with this heart of mine?
Naught see I fixed or sure in thee!
I do not know thee,—nor what deeds are thine:
Love, love, what will though with this heart of mine?
Shall I be mute, or vows with prayers combine?
Ye who are blessed in loving, tell it me:
Love, love, what wilt thou with this heart of mine?
Naught see I permanent or sure in thee!

As you can hear, although a triolet is eight lines, it is essentially an amplified couplet (two lines of poetry). This is because the first two lines are repeated at the end of the eight-line poem, their two rhyme-sounds carry the entire poem, and there is an additional repetition of the first line in the middle of the poem (fourth line). Thus, an echoing, chant-like resonance flourishes a single couplet of poetry. If you have an excellent couplet but feel there is more to it, and yet nothing more to it than just two lines, then consider this form.

Here's a triolet I wrote:

Ephemera

by Carol Smallwood

Mayflies bear a Greek name meaning living a day,
An allusion to their dance before they die
After maturing in the month of May.
Mayflies bear a Greek name meaning living a day
And start as water nymphs that grow to fly
Only to die after mating—a last hooray.
Mayflies bear a Greek name meaning living a day,
An allusion to their dance before they die.

2.7 How to Write in Terza Rima

by Dusty Grein

DATING TO THE 13th century, the terza rima (Italian for "third rhyme") is a classic form of writing poetry in three-line stanzas called tercets, which are interlinked by their rhyming pattern. They use the ending sound from each tercet's middle line, as the first and third of the next, creating the pattern aba, bcb, cdc, ded, and so on. There is no limit to the number of tercet stanzas that can be used.

The terza rima is often credited to the Italian poet Dante Alighieri (1265–1321). He was the first to use the form to create a popular recorded epic, *The Divine Comedy*, but it was probably based on tercet poems and songs performed by the Provençal troubadours of his day.

Geoffrey Chaucer introduced the terza rima to England with his poem "A Complaint to His Lady," but it was truly popularized by Thomas Wyatt through both translations and original works. It became a favorite style for many of the English Romantic poets of the 19th century.

Meter

Originally, terza rimas were written in 11-syllable lines (hendecasyllable); however, any meter can be used as long as it is consistent throughout. Most written in English are composed using iambic lines, with either pentameter or tetrameter being the most common.

Some classical poets have taken liberties and split the stanzas into mixed sets or combined them all into one long nonstanzaic work, but the rhyme scheme is retained. Here is the opening excerpt from one of Lord Byron's terza rimas:

Francesca of Rimini

by Lord Byron ((1788–1824)

"The Land where I was born sits by the Seas
Upon that shore to which the Po descends,
With all his followers, in search of peace.
Love, which the gentle heart soon apprehends,
Seized him for the fair person which was ta'en
From me, and me even yet the mode offends.
Love, who to none beloved to love again
Remits, seized me with wish to please, so strong,
That, as thou see'st, yet, yet it doth remain."

Subforms

Many poets have used terza rima architecture to create small and complete forms unto themselves. The two most popular of these are probably the terza rima sonnet and the terzanelle.

The poet Percy Bysshe Shelley (1792–1822) wrote his "Ode to the West Wind" as a set of five cantos (a canto is like a chapter in a long poem), and each was a 14-line open sonnet (aba, bcb, cdc, ded, ee), consisting of four linked tercets in terza rima and a couplet. One of the most well-known closed sonnets written using tercets is from the 20th-century poet Robert Frost. A closed sonnet means that the final rhyme repeats the first rhyme. The rhyme pattern for Frost's closed sonnet below is Aba, bcb, cdc, dad, aA. The first and last lines receive a capital A because they are exactly the same line:

Acquainted with the Night

by Robert Frost (1874–1963)

I have been one acquainted with the night.
I have walked out in rain—and back in rain.
I have outwalked the furthest city light.

I have looked down the saddest city lane.
I have passed by the watchman on his beat
And dropped my eyes, unwilling to explain.

I have stood still and stopped the sound of feet
When far away an interrupted cry
Came over houses from another street,

But not to call me back or say good-bye;
And further still at an unearthly height,
One luminary clock against the sky

Proclaimed the time was neither wrong nor right
I have been one acquainted with the night.

Modern classical poets have combined the terza rima with the villanelle to create a new form known as a terzanelle. This 19-line poetry form uses five interwoven terza rima tercets and a quatrain, using the first and third lines as the final two, as in a villanelle (see Section 2.4 How to Write a Villanelle on page 65.) Here is an example of the terzanelle:

Loud Today

by Dusty Grein

The voices in my head are loud today,
I plug my ears, but still I hear them talk
Oh please, oh please just make them go away!

I thought that maybe I could take a walk
That they would quiet down and let me think
I plug my ears, but still I hear them talk

I'm trying not to let my spirit sink,
These voices drowning out my fervent plea
That they would quiet down and let me think

I hear them use my mouth. That wasn't me!
Oh please help me ignore their foul demands
These voices drowning out my fervent plea

I hang my head, then fiercely wring my hands
As they tell me to do such evil things
Oh please help me ignore their foul demands

Pure misery their constant echoes bring,
As they tell me to do such evil things
The voices in my head are loud today,
Oh please, oh please just make them go away!

Writing Your Own

Whether you prefer the open-ended structure first used by Dante, the closed sonnet preferred by Frost, or the newer terzanelle, the crafting of a terza rima poem is not difficult. I will show you, step by step, my own method for crafting a closed terza rima sonnet.

Some poets prefer to fly by the seat of the pants, but I tend to build a skeleton to hang my poems on first, and then fill in and adjust as necessary.

The first step, as always, is to choose your subject matter. I often find my inspiration in images, so knowing I wanted to dig deep into an emotion, I found an image of a man walking away into the fog on a wooded path, and it screamed "grief" to me. Whatever method you use to find the message you wish to convey poetically, you must decide how to proceed, but I suggest you let your feelings lead the way.

Next you must decide on your meter. Most English sonnets, standard or terza rima, are written using iambic pentameter, but in tribute to the original form, I am going to use a hendecasyllable meter, specifically amphibrachic tetrameter catalectic (see Section 2.3 The Mechanics of Classical Poetry on page 59).

Now is the most difficult part of the process for me, and that is choosing the first line. This will also be the last line for a closed poem, so it must be able to be used to open and close the work. This is where your poetic talent, skill, and experience come into play.

After some thought, my opening (and closing) line will be "In solitude I roamed a mist shrouded path."

Now I choose my rhyming words, by finding sets of words that bring to my mind an emotional response or the possibility of creating one. I need four sets of three words, and each must end with a strong stressed syllable. My first set is my "A" rhyme, which I know must rhyme with "path." Here then are the words I chose to use:

> A – wrath, bath, hath
> B – sound, bound, found
> C – gray, pray, away
> D – gloom, bloom, doom

Now I can use the basic 14-line framework to insert these rhymes into tercets, with my first and last line in place. Note that in the following frame, (–) is a soft, unstressed syllable and (=) is a hard, stressed one:

> (A1) In solitude I roamed a mist shrouded path
> (b) – = – | – = – | – = – | – sound
> (a) – = – | – = – | – = – | – wrath
> (b) – = – | – = – | – = – | – bound
> (c) – = – | – = – | – = – | – gray
> (b) – = – | – = – | – = – | – found
> (c) – = – | – = – | – = – | – pray
> (d) – = – | – = – | – = – | – gloom
> (c) – = – | – = – | – = – | away

(d) – = – | – = – | – = – | – bloom
(a) – = – | – = – | – = – | – bath
(d) – = – | – = – | – = – | – doom
(d) – = – | – = – | – = – | – hath
(A1) In solitude I roamed a mist shrouded path.

At this point you must use your tools to sculpt your creation into life, using whatever meter you have chosen. In this case, it is the one-TWO-three, one-TWO-three cadence of the amphibrach. If you find as you work that a particular word doesn't work, you simply replace it with one that does. Here then is my finalized poem:

A Mist Shrouded Path

by Dusty Grein

In solitude I roamed a mist shrouded path
Where icy fog soon devoured every sound
A victim of all my fears and heaven's wrath.

In my heart this sharp pain was carefully bound,
My feet carried me deeper into the gray
As if some enlightenment there could be found.

Near a spectral tree I stopped, kneeling to pray;
as answer there came to me naught but deep gloom.
In anger, I'd cast my faith blindly away.

After losing them before new life could bloom,
Grief flooded my soul with its poisonous bath.
The silent fog now verified my life's doom.

Avoiding the pain that my poor heart now hath,
In solitude I roamed a mist shrouded path.

I quite like the result, and may just use this poem in my own Collected Works. If you try it, you may just find that you enjoy crafting poetry in terza rima style as well.

2.8 How to Write a Limerick

by Dusty Grein

THE HISTORY OF the poetry form we know as the limerick is rich and wild. There are examples of the limerick's cadence and pattern in use as early as the 11th century, and Shakespeare used the form and meter as part of a few of his plays, including as a drinking song in his play *The Tempest*. In 1776, at the time of the American Revolution, the form was used quite extensively in the first published version of *Mother Goose's Melodies*. "Little Miss Muffet" has since affixed the metrical pattern into a recognized tempo for most children, worldwide.

If you look, you will find many different opinions on origins of the use of the name. It is quite clear that there is a historical connection between the nonsense-verse style and the county of the same name in Ireland. It was there that the creation of drinking songs using the metrical beat and rhyme pattern gained popularity, and the name Limerick was first used to denote the poetry as a form in 1898.

The popularity of the limerick in its current form can be traced back to the poet Edward Lear (1812–1888) in *A Book of Nonsense*, written in 1845, and a second book he wrote in 1872. Lear wrote over 200 of these rhymes in the two books, and most of them were nonsensical and humorous—which is still true of the form today.

The Structure

Limericks are one of the more loosely defined forms of classical poetry, and are written using a variety of metric feet, but they do have a commonly accepted rhythm and pattern that separates them from other five-line, or quintain, forms, such as the tanka or the cinquain.

Having a looser definition means that limericks, which may be acatalectic (having perfectly formed metric feet), quite often are not.

Their meter is frequently adjusted to make the rhyming pattern fit. The addition of an extra syllable at either end of the lines can make them hypercatalectic, or they may be catalectic and have missing syllables at one end or the other.

The most common limericks use a three-beat foot, typically either the anapest (dee-dee-DUM) or the amphibrach (dee-DUM-dee). These are built into trimeters for lines 1 and 2, dimeters for lines 3 and 4, and a trimeter again for the fifth and final line.

The final defining structural piece of the form is the rhyming pattern of ABCCB or AABBA.

Content

From its historical roots as a drinking song to the silliness encouraged by both Mother Goose and Edward Lear, the limerick has developed a reputation of being generally humorous, and very often being risqué, bawdy, and even sexually suggestive.

The limerick is also quite often crafted using the name of a place at the end of the first line—and in the case of poets like Edward Lear, that same place name was repeated at the end of line 5, as in this poem from his first book:

> There was a Young Person of Smyrna,
> Whose Grandmother threatened to burn her;
> But she seized on the cat,
> And said, 'Granny, burn that!
> You incongruous Old Woman of Smyrna!'
> —from *A Book of Nonsense*

Writing Your Own

Designing a limerick isn't difficult, but constructing one that is humorous, without delving into material that is unsuitable for family audiences, can be a challenge. Like a well-timed joke, a funny limerick is not as easy to create as it may seem at first, but if you are careful and you work at the task, it can be done.

The basic structure of the limerick can be presented using the dash symbol (–) for the soft syllables, the equal sign (=) for the hard ones, and the vertical bar (|) to separate the metric feet. This gives us the following framework:

```
– = – | – = – | – = –
– = – | – = – | – = –
– = – | – = –
– = – | – = –
– = – | – = – | – = –
```

The first step, for me, is to think of a humorous image. Knowing that stereotypes and tropes often make the best humor, I decided to use the image of a nagging wife who loses her voice and makes her husband happy.

Now I need to find my rhyming words. In order to make it easier on myself, I create a final line for the rhyme first: "I have never found you more delightful!"

My next step is to find a pair of rhyming words that fit into the image I am creating, and toward this end I chose "frightful" (because that's what nagging is) and "insightful" because it rhymes and the comment could be thought of as such. I was then struck by the fact that if her voice "died" then his comment might be one he "cried."

I then place these words into the framework:

```
– = – | – = – | – frightful,
– = – | – = – | insightful.
– = – | – died,
– = – | – cried
```
"I have never found you more delightful!"

From here, it is simply a matter of plugging in words to complete the lines. This is easier with limericks than some other forms, because of the nature of the form and the fact that we can freestyle the syllable requirements a bit.

In the end, here is what I wrote:

A Limerick

by Dusty Grein

A man whose wife's nagging was frightful,
Made a comment I found quite insightful ...
   One day her voice died,
   and he joyfully cried,
"I have never found you more delightful!"

Okay, it probably won't win any awards, but I found it to be funny. As limericks go, it isn't the worst one I have ever read, and it is clean, clear, and made me smile.

   I hope you have enjoyed this little exercise, and I would encourage you all to give your best shot at one—but let's keep it suitable for family viewing!

2.9 How to Write a Rubaiyat

by Sathya Narayana

THE RUBAIYAT (PRONOUNCED "roo-bái-yát") is a Persian poetic form consisting of several quatrains. Its name is derived from the Arabic plural of the word for "quatrain," rubá'íyah. This, in turn, comes from the Arabic word rubá, meaning "four." A rubai (the singular form) is a quatrain or a set of two couplets.

The rubai form is more than a thousand years old. The rubaiyat was created by a non-Arab poet by the name Abul Hassan Rodeki. But the rubaiyat form was later taken to glorified heights by Omar Khayyam (1048–1131), a great Persian poet, astronomer, philosopher, and mathematician. Khayyam, lovelorn, became addicted to wine and, inspired by his memories of his estranged lover, he composed a number of beautiful rubaiyat, filled with love, pain, philosophy, and the panacean benefits of wine. His rubaiyat were translated into a number of languages, including English. Here is an example of Khayyam's rubaiyat well-translated by the 19th-century English poet Edward Fitzgerald (a close friend of the celebrated poet laureate Alfred, Lord Tennyson):

Rubaiyat

by Omar Khayyam

The Moving Finger writes; and, having writ,
Moves on: nor all thy Piety nor Wit,
Shall lure it back to cancel half a Line,
Nor all thy Tears wash out a Word of it.

But helpless pieces in the game He plays,
Upon this chequer-board of Nights and Days,
He hither and thither moves, and checks ... and slays,
Then one by one, back in the Closet lays.

And, as the Cock crew, those who stood before
The Tavern shouted—"Open then the Door!
You know how little time we have to stay,
And once departed, may return no more."

A Book of Verses underneath the Bough,
A Jug of Wine, a Loaf of Bread—and Thou,
Beside me singing in the Wilderness,
And oh, Wilderness is Paradise enow.

Myself when young did eagerly frequent
Doctor and Saint, and heard great Argument
About it and about: but evermore
Came out of the same Door as in I went.

Rubaiyat in English

The English adaptation of the rubaiyat is equally beautiful and well-suited to modern thought, imagery, and muse. In a single rubaiyat stanza, the rhyme scheme of aaba is used with enjambment (the continuing of a sentence or thought) between the third and fourth lines. Here is an example of a rubaiyat by the famous American poet Robert Frost in iambic tetrameter with a deviation of rhyme order in the last stanza (dddd):

Stopping by Woods on a Snowy Evening

by Robert Frost (1874–1963)

Whose woods these are I think I know.
His house is in the village though;
He will not see me stopping here
To watch his woods fill up with snow.

My little horse must think it queer
To stop without a farmhouse near
Between the woods and frozen lake
The darkest evening of the year.

He gives his harness bells a shake
To ask if there is some mistake.
The only other sound's the sweep
Of easy wind and downy flake.

The woods are lovely, dark and deep,
But I have promises to keep,
And miles to go before I sleep,
And miles to go before I sleep.

Modern poets also compose rubaiyat in iambic pentameter. The above poem is also an example of an interlocking rubaiyat in which the subsequent stanza rhymes its first, second, and fourth lines with the sound at the end of the third line in the stanza before it.

Note that the rubaiyat is allowed an unlimited number of stanzas, so extend or shorten the pattern as needed: For example, the contemporary poet Bernard M. Jackson preferred to only use three quatrains. The rhyming order for a three-stanza rubaiyat, in theory, is aaba bbcb ccdc. This standard pattern cracks in the concluding stanza, since the third line always assumes the same rhyme ending as that of the third line of the previous stanza, and the "d" sound here has no following stanza with which to rhyme. A solution to this crack, which is employed by Jackson in his poem below, is to return the third line of the final stanza to the primary rhyme of the first stanza, creating a beautiful and contemplative circular structure. For example, the rhyme scheme in Jackson's three-stanza rubaiyat below is as follows: aaba bbcb ccac

To a Lasting Dream

by Bernard M. Jackson

Down fleeting years Time's shades have swiftly flown
Though seasoned joys we never have outgrown;
Besides some rippled brook now let us lie,
To muse upon fond moments we have known.

Sweet fragrance of rare bloom still draws a sigh,
So, too, those woodland haunts we lingered by.
Each summer traces paths of former ways
With welcome spell of dreams that never die.

Thus sipped from fate with gladness, all our days,
There's nothing may love's memories erase;
Eternal are the visitors Time has shown,
As life slips through each measures passing phase.

Here is another example of a four-stanza rubaiyat composed by me.

Affluence

by Sathya Narayana

The dark muddy puddles on road, by rain
can't bring, I thought, the times bygone again.
My latest home in town's posh colony
has well buried my past travails and pain.

The days I whined and ran with agony;
the days I starved and craved for small money;
no more exist in memory. I laid
a lid on that dramatic irony.

For great windfall I gained of late, I bade
good bye to mates, for me, who cried and prayed.
Forgot the days I drank rice-soup in grange
with friends and pools in which we splashed and played.

Better were days of need than these deranged
in binge, in spite of piled fancy mélange.
My food tastes sour; and bitter my Champagne.
I got riches; from me but sleep estranged.

2.10 How to Write a Poem Like 'The Raven'

by Dusty Grein

"THE RAVEN" BY Edgar Allan Poe remains one of the English language's most popular and influential poems since it was written in 1845. Much of this was Poe's own doing, as he performed it quite frequently and wrote many essays and commentaries on it in the press. It has cemented itself in the modern era and has been the subject of many portrayals, from Vincent Price in the 1960s to the *Simpsons* rendition in the 1990s.

One of the keys to its incredible appeal is its brilliant rhyme pattern and rhythm. While the language may be somewhat difficult to understand or relate to, people keep returning to it for Poe's enchanting classical meter.

We are going to take a look at the poem itself, explore its rhythmic genius in depth, and discuss using this poetic framework to build a poem of our own.

The Poem

In an early draft of the poem, Poe actually had a parrot instead of a raven. This gives us some basic idea of what is going on throughout this poem. A man is sitting in his study late at night when he hears knocking. He opens the door, but no one is there. After more knocking, he opens the window and a raven flies in, seeking shelter from the stormy night. It then begins repeating the same word over and over again: "nevermore."

In an otherwise realistic poem, this slight supernatural flourish creates just the right amount of mystery to push the story along as we learn about the narrator's lost love, Lenore, who will return "nevermore." The bird's echoed mutterings to the questions he asks make him feel even worse in his melancholy.

Not exactly a brilliant plot, but it's a study in deep emotion and a vehicle for vigorous language. It poignantly and beautifully depicts the haunting feeling of longing one has for a love that is distant or lost.

Useful vocabulary when reading the poem:

Pallas: Another name for Athena, Greek goddess of wisdom and war.

Plutonian: Derived from Pluto. Another name for Hades, which refers to both the Kingdom of the Dead and the god of the Dead.

Seraphim: Six-winged angels.

Nepenthe: An ancient medicine for relieving sorrow, originating from Egypt.

Balm in Gilead: A rare medicinal perfume mentioned in the Bible that has come to represent a cure-all.

Aidenn: The Garden of Eden; paradise in a general sense.

This version is a direct reprint, retaining the original spelling, approved by Poe himself.

The Raven

by Edgar Allan Poe (1809–1849)

Once upon a midnight dreary, while I pondered, weak and weary,
Over many a quaint and curious volume of forgotten lore —
While I nodded, nearly napping, suddenly there came a tapping,
As of some one gently rapping, rapping at my chamber door.
" 'Tis some visiter," I muttered, "tapping at my chamber door —
Only this and nothing more."

Ah, distinctly I remember it was in the bleak December;
And each separate dying ember wrought its ghost upon the floor.
Eagerly I wished the morrow; — vainly I had sought to borrow
From my books surcease of sorrow — sorrow for the lost Lenore —
For the rare and radiant maiden whom the angels name Lenore —
Nameless here for evermore.

And the silken, sad, uncertain rustling of each purple curtain
Thrilled me — filled me with fantastic terrors never felt before;
So that now, to still the beating of my heart, I stood repeating

" 'Tis some visiter entreating entrance at my chamber door —
Some late visiter entreating entrance at my chamber door; —
This it is and nothing more."

Presently my soul grew stronger; hesitating then no longer,
"Sir," said I, "or Madam, truly your forgiveness I implore;
But the fact is I was napping, and so gently you came rapping,
And so faintly you came tapping, tapping at my chamber door,
That I scarce was sure I heard you" — here I opened wide the door; —
Darkness there and nothing more.

Deep into that darkness peering, long I stood there wondering, fearing,
Doubting, dreaming dreams no mortal ever dared to dream before;
But the silence was unbroken, and the stillness gave no token,
And the only word there spoken was the whispered word, "Lenore?"
This I whispered, and an echo murmured back the word, "Lenore!" —
Merely this and nothing more.

Back into the chamber turning, all my soul within me burning,
Soon again I heard a tapping somewhat louder than before.
"Surely," said I, "surely that is something at my window lattice;
Let me see, then, what thereat is, and this mystery explore —
Let my heart be still a moment and this mystery explore; —
'Tis the wind and nothing more!"

Open here I flung the shutter, when, with many a flirt and flutter,
In there stepped a stately Raven of the saintly days of yore;
Not the least obeisance made he; not a minute stopped or stayed he;
But, with mien of lord or lady, perched above my chamber door —
Perched upon a bust of Pallas just above my chamber door —
Perched, and sat, and nothing more.

Then this ebony bird beguiling my sad fancy into smiling,
By the grave and stern decorum of the countenance it wore,
"Though thy crest be shorn and shaven, thou," I said, "art sure no craven,
Ghastly grim and ancient Raven wandering from the Nightly shore —
Tell me what thy lordly name is on the Night's Plutonian shore!"
Quoth the Raven "Nevermore."

Much I marvelled this ungainly fowl to hear discourse so plainly,
Though its answer little meaning — little relevancy bore;
For we cannot help agreeing that no living human being
Ever yet was blessed with seeing bird above his chamber door —
Bird or beast upon the sculptured bust above his chamber door,
With such name as "Nevermore."

But the Raven, sitting lonely on the placid bust, spoke only
That one word, as if his soul in that one word he did outpour.
Nothing farther then he uttered — not a feather then he fluttered —
Till I scarcely more than muttered "Other friends have flown before —
On the morrow he will leave me, as my Hopes have flown before."
Then the bird said "Nevermore."

Startled at the stillness broken by reply so aptly spoken,
"Doubtless," said I, "what it utters is its only stock and store
Caught from some unhappy master whom unmerciful Disaster
Followed fast and followed faster till his songs one burden bore —
Till the dirges of his Hope that melancholy burden bore
Of 'Never — nevermore'."

But the Raven still beguiling my sad fancy into smiling,
Straight I wheeled a cushioned seat in front of bird, and bust and door;
Then, upon the velvet sinking, I betook myself to linking
Fancy unto fancy, thinking what this ominous bird of yore —
What this grim, ungainly, ghastly, gaunt, and ominous bird of yore
Meant in croaking "Nevermore."

This I sat engaged in guessing, but no syllable expressing
To the fowl whose fiery eyes now burned into my bosom's core;
This and more I sat divining, with my head at ease reclining
On the cushion's velvet lining that the lamp-light gloated o'er,
But whose velvet-violet lining with the lamp-light gloating o'er,
She shall press, ah, nevermore!

Then, methought, the air grew denser, perfumed from an unseen censer
Swung by seraphim whose foot-falls tinkled on the tufted floor.
"Wretch," I cried, "thy God hath lent thee — by these angels he hath sent
   thee
Respite — respite and nepenthe, from thy memories of Lenore;
Quaff, oh quaff this kind nepenthe and forget this lost Lenore!"
Quoth the Raven "Nevermore."

"Prophet!" said I, "thing of evil! — prophet still, if bird or devil! —
Whether Tempter sent, or whether tempest tossed thee here ashore,
Desolate yet all undaunted, on this desert land enchanted —
On this home by Horror haunted — tell me truly, I implore —
Is there — is there balm in Gilead? — tell me — tell me, I implore!"
Quoth the Raven "Nevermore."

"Prophet!" said I, "thing of evil! — prophet still, if bird or devil!
By that Heaven that bends above us — by that God we both adore —
Tell this soul with sorrow laden if, within the distant Aidenn,
It shall clasp a sainted maiden whom the angels name Lenore —
Clasp a rare and radiant maiden whom the angels name Lenore."
Quoth the Raven "Nevermore."

"Be that word our sign of parting, bird or fiend!" I shrieked, upstarting —
"Get thee back into the tempest and the Night's Plutonian shore!
Leave no black plume as a token of that lie thy soul hath spoken!
Leave my loneliness unbroken! — quit the bust above my door!
Take thy beak from out my heart, and take thy form from off my door!"
Quoth the Raven "Nevermore."

And the Raven, never flitting, still is sitting, still is sitting
On the pallid bust of Pallas just above my chamber door;
And his eyes have all the seeming of a demon's that is dreaming,
And the lamp-light o'er him streaming throws his shadow on the floor;
And my soul from out that shadow that lies floating on the floor
Shall be lifted — nevermore!

Deciphering the Meter of "The Raven"

Quick review from Section 2.3 (page 60): A trochee is a two-syllable foot consisting of a hard syllable followed by a soft one—the opposite of an iamb—and trochaic lines are built from these trochees. A tetrameter is a set of four poetic feet, and an octameter is eight poetic feet.

Poe was a skilled craftsman of the English language. His mastery of difficult poetry is evident here in the use of trochaic octameter. He himself published an essay, "The Philosophy of Composition," regarding the methodical process he used to create his poem. In it, he explains, step by step, how "The Raven" came to be, and the logic behind each image and emotion.

Instead of focusing on these creative decisions and the philosophy that is expressed through the process, I would like to discuss the mechanics behind the poetic architecture of the piece. It is the one area that Poe only lightly touches on, and this structure—if followed closely—will help the aspiring poet to build a narrative poem, based on whatever subject he or she desires, with a melodic cadence and flow.

The poem itself was created in trochaic syllable pairs, instead of iambic ones, and each stanza consists of 11 tetrameters. These are welded together into five octameter lines, followed by the final refrain-like tetrameter line, the raven's immortal quote and that ominous long "OR" sound.

Poe also used the subtle trick of omitting the final syllable on lines 2, 4, 5, and 6, which all rhyme. This method is called catalectic (headless), and emphasizes these lines by letting the final syllable stand alone.

Finally, the poem was built using a very strict rhyming pattern as follows:

AA,

xB,

CC,

CB,

xB,

B

Adding to the difficulty of this masterpiece, is the fact that the same refrain rhyme syllable (the B in the pattern) is used in all 18 stanzas of the poem.

To clarify, let's look at the structure of the poem ("x" means that no rhyme is needed):

[A A] Once upon a midnight *dreary*, while I pondered, weak and *weary*,
[x B] Over many a quaint and *curious* volume of forgotten *lore* —
[C C] While I nodded, nearly *napping*, suddenly there came a *tapping*,
[C B] As of some one gently *rapping*, rapping at my chamber *door*.
[x B] "'Tis some visiter," I *muttered*, "tapping at my chamber *door* —
[B] Only this and nothing *more*."

If you read just the italicized words—the fourth trochee in each tetrametered half-line—you will see the inherent flow of the piece.

Creating a Poem, Following This Pattern

Building a poem on this frame presents us with some challenges. First let's break down the number of rhyming words:

"A" words: We need at least two of these rhyming words, which must end with a trochee (two syllables, with the first one stressed). I like the challenge of finding three of these words that rhyme, and using the third one in line 2, in place of the "x" word, treating it like the "C" words in lines 3 and 4.

"C" words: We need three of these. Like the "A" words, these three rhyming words must end in a trochee, and are easiest to do with two-syllable words.

"B" words: Here is the true challenge. We need four rhyming words, of a single stressed syllable. These will replace the eighth trochee at the end of lines 2, 4, 5 and the fourth at the end of line 6.

"x" words: Here for use in line 5 (and line 2 if you desire) is our connecting trochee, as the fourth of eight in the line. This trochee does not have to rhyme, although I like to make the one in line 2 an "A" rhyme. Poe sometimes does this, and other times does not.

An Example

This style of poem lends itself quite well to stories that are supernatural or terrifying, although it could express emotions in any genre. For the purposes of this exercise, we will create an example using fear to create a mood.

I once saw an image of several bodies floating in the air above an old weed-covered yard, and it is the image I will convey through the example stanza. Following Poe's framework, I will use three "A" words, three "C" words, and four "B" words. I will use a single "x" tie-in trochee for line 5. Here then are the words I selected, chosen for rhyme, and mood:

3 "A" words: wander, ponder, yonder (Note that these are all trochees.)
3 "C" words: tighten, whiten, frighten(ed) (Again, all trochees.)
4 "B" words: see, flee, free, me (These are all single hard syllables.)

Using the pattern, we will now write out the framework of our piece, using = for the hard syllables, and _ for the soft ones with each trochee, and inserting our selected words:

= – = – = – wander = – = – = – ponder ____(total syllables: 16)
= – = – = – yonder = – = – = – see _____(total syllables: 15)
= – = – = – tighten = – = – = – whiten _____(total syllables: 16)
= – = – = – frightened = – = – = – flee _____(total syllables: 15)
= – = – = – = – = – = – = – free _____(total syllables: 15)
= – = – = – me_____(total syllables: 7)

Here is where creativity and imagination as a poet truly express themselves. Keeping the meter in mind, we build the lines by inserting three trochees in front of each previously selected word, and a single tie-in trochee in line 5.

Here is a stanza I created, built onto this framework:

Cautiously at night I wander through the moonlight, there to ponder
On the shapes that hang but yonder, at the edge of what I see.
Fearfully my muscles tighten and my face begins to whiten;
Though I try not to be frightened, 'tis a battle not to flee.
In the darkness something flutters, struggling, trying to get free—
In the dark, calling to me.

There you go. The creation of a single stanza of a narrative poem, written in structured catalectic trochaic octameter. Sounds a lot more complicated than it really is. Edgar Allen Poe wrote his epic poem using 18 stanzas, 108 lines, to tell the story of "The Raven"— but then he was a true master.

Poems Similar to "The Raven"

Many people list "The Raven" as their favorite poem, and their interest in poetry ends there. They hear or read some free verse, which lacks clear rhyming or rhythm, and sadly for some, the attraction to poetry is over.

If you like "The Raven," but don't really care for free-verse poetry, don't lose hope! There are many other poems that have similar classical meter. In particular, the following poem has a rhythm very similar to that of "The Raven":

The Falun Gong Practitioner

inspired by the real and ongoing persecution of peaceful Falun Gong practitioners today in China

by Evan Mantyk

Not that long ago in China, in a labor camp confined a
Year or longer, I was sitting, making for a U.S. store
Christmas tree lights meant for hanging, when there came an awful banging
Like a phantom's chains' loud clanging—angling through the metal door.
As the banging and the clanging entered upon the room's floor,
I recalled what came before:

I'd been peacefully posed there standing, my mind tranquilly expanding
When suddenly police with cuffs and clubs came for us in scores,
Telling us that "Faith renouncing, is the only way convincing,
That you'll have for your releasing, walking out the metal door."
I said "No" and they tried beating out the beliefs at my core—
But I said, "No" evermore.

Hanging me from arms back twisted, as long as my faith persisted,
Slapping until my bright red blood turned maroon upon the floor.
Then they brought batons electric, shooting out blue claws frenetic
Caused my body to go spastic, as their tools upon me bore.
Later when they threw on water, and they asked "Do you want more?"
I stayed silent evermore.

Many long days and nights followed, deep in misery I wallowed,
Thinking, "For what do I deserve conditions I so deplore?"
Then an order came for shipping, as my stamina was slipping,
My collar the guard was gripping, griping at me to "Work more!"
Six-month sentence expired; they asked if my faith I could deplore?
I stayed silent evermore.

Dreary thoughts like these came flooding, stale and broken visions brooding
As awful banging and loud clanging came through the metal door.
The policeman came in bringing long strange pieces he was flinging
Something he'd been rearranging, fixing up to make some more
Christmas packaging, improving our productivity score.
I stayed silent evermore.

Dollar signs in eyes came flashing, around the room he was dashing
Eager to see it operating upon the camp's squalid floor.

Meanwhile my hands kept on working, his police baton kept lurking
Until I saw the thing jerking, working to improve our score.
Then he was spitting, "We can double our quota and work more!"
I stayed silent evermore.

My hands suddenly stopped moving, gently stopped us from "improving,"
As I had seen some brave labor camp prisoners do before.
Then a guard came at me quickly, waving his club, looking strictly,
But was failing to break me, knock me down upon the floor.
The head guard came over, hit me, and asked "Do you want more?"
I said, "I'll work nevermore."

Now his fury flared insanely, with a rod hit me painfully,
Down I bent but did not crumble upon the camp's squalid floor.
Two guards locked me in a tank cell, filled with sewage that stank like hell,
If off my toes I sank or fell into that filthy pungent shore—
I feared I would lose my mind, yet I shouted out from my core:
"Falun Gong forevermore!"

Finally they left me hanging like some Christmas lights dangling,
Limply swaying back and forth all lit up with bloodstains and sores,
Until the leader came raging, filled with lies that were deranging,
Lies the media were staging, propagandizing galore,
Poison causing people to hate meditators more and more.
Then my lips breathed nevermore.

Seeing my body's not breathing, and anger no longer seething,
The guard, a policeman, said, "Pick her up off the squalid floor.
We don't want the fam'ly suing, so I'll tell you what we'll be doing,
We'll say 'twas her own misdoing: doing what people deplore,
Committing suicide just so she didn't have to finish her chores.
(Cremate so none can explore.)"

Just the moment my heart beating, ceased its rhythmic repeating,
The head guard's bruised wife and daughter walked out their apartment
        door,
Saying, "I'm never returning, for life without him I'm yearning;
Hopefully he'll be discerning, learning that a woman's not for
Only swearing at and slapping around when she doesn't do a chore;
Of that I will have no more."

The machine the camp was running, which could make profits stunning
Would in six months turn one guard's right hand into a mess of gore,
Creating a bad infection not stopped by any injection;
Doctors cut off the whole section of the rotten arm that bore

Batons electric against those who passed through the metal door,
Whose blood his joined on the floor.

One guard with bad constipation, soon would feel a sharp sensation.
Running to the toilet, but before he passed the metal door,
Filth the bottom spews usually, came out of his mouth profusely,
Seeming to come unceasingly spread out on the squalid floor.
Not so unusually, dysentery was what he had in store,
He died in one year, not more.

When the last light in my brown eyes, was extinguished without reprise
All the Christmas tree lights I had made that had been shipped to stores—
Stores across China locally, Europe and U.S. globally—
Acting in solidarity, died and shined their light no more,
Mimicking the darkness upon the labor camp's squalid floor
Where my eyes shined nevermore.

Meanwhile my soul was raising, into radiant encasing
Woven of the fine material released from my inner core
Into matter-mind confluence, where ideas have real substance;
Where thought can make a difference; the sixth sense real as the floor;
Where the Truth, Compassion, and Tolerance that were my faith's lore
Came alive and made me soar.
.
I flew upward and was greeted, by divine beings, some seated,
Having arrived at Heaven's breath-taking iridescent shore,
Where the beings' magnificence, their halos' profound resplendence,
Their nimbus's soft elegance, entranced my mind evermore,
But, one such great being told me, "You can't enter Heaven's door,
For you to do there's still more."

I was sent back to Earth's setting as a spirit tasked with spreading
Wisdom at various aisles of your local department store,
Showing third-eye-open children the labor camp a toy had been
By innocent slaves produced in—such sin, misery, and gore
That the plastic doll or truck dropped to the glistening floor,
Children crying, "Nevermore."

Floating invisible goddess with ancient and modern prowess,
I inspire life without Made-in-China gadgets anymore;
Through greeting cards of cherubs 'n angels, Buddha statues in décor aisles,
Through garden chimes' gentle tingles, jingles of Santa's sled door,
Spreading a message of morals and those great kingdoms of yore,
Which live on forevermore.

2.11 How to Write a Pantoum

by Carol Smallwood

THE PANTOUM IS a poetry form that originated in 15th-century Malaysia and drifted West in the 19th century with French writer Victor Hugo, among others. While it never quite took off like the haiku, it never fully went away either and has been steadily blossoming among English poets.

Unlike the 14-line sonnet, pantoums do not have to be a certain length. The challenge comes with the repetition of two lines from the first stanza in the following stanza. Additionally, in the traditional pantoum form that I prefer, the first line becomes the last line and the third line becomes the third from last. The payoff of a well-executed pantoum is a picture-like poem that seems to dance in circles outside the boundaries of time.

This is the format I use:

Stanza 1:
4 lines, ABAB rhyme scheme

Stanza 2:
Line 5 (repeat of line 2 in stanza 1)
Line 6 (new line)
Line 7 (repeat of line 4 in stanza 1)
Line 8 (new line)

Stanza 3:
Last Stanza (This is the format for the last stanza regardless of how many preceding stanzas exist):
Line 9   (line 2 of the previous stanza)
Line 10 (line 3 of the first stanza)
Line 11 (line 4 of the previous stanza)
Line 12 (line 1 of the first stanza)

As with other formal poems, one must not let the form drive the poem and should select topics carefully: Like when Goldilocks is looking for a bed in the three bears' house, it must be just right.

Here is an example of a pantoum:

Tongue-Tied

by Susan Jarvis Bryant

The powers that be declare our speech is free,
As long as words are PC and benign
And parrot propaganda endlessly—
The shining vision of the party line.

As long as words are PC and benign,
They'll bless us with their just and ideal view—
The shining vision of the party line—
Utopia, a world God can't outdo.

They'll bless us with their just and ideal view,
Endowed with virtues lesser gospels lack—
Utopia, a world God can't outdo,
Will kick each heretic straight back on track.

Endowed with virtues lesser gospels lack,
Their doctrine, honed and polished to the hilt,
Will kick each heretic straight back on track
By praising crooks and tainting saints with guilt.

Their doctrine's honed and polished to the hilt.
Their tone is tuned to twist the truth with lies.
By praising crooks and tainting saints with guilt
They cancel out the curious and wise.

Their tone is tuned to twist the truth with lies
And parrot propaganda endlessly.
While canceling the curious and wise,
The powers that be declare our speech is free.

2.12 How to Write a Sestina

by Dusty Grein

THE SESTINA ORIGINATED among the troubadours of medieval France's Provence region, and the modern 39-line form is attributed to one of these traveling poet entertainers of the 12th century, Arnaut Daniel. Daniel's sestina form was admired by Dante Alighieri, who introduced it to Italian poetry as well.

The sestina is one of the more challenging forms of the era, and perhaps that is one reason it is also a very fulfilling form to craft a poem in—especially when it comes together well. Like many French forms, such as the villanelle and the triolet, the sestina is very strictly patterned. Unlike these other forms, however, the sestina in its original form was not written using rhymes. Instead, it uses a set of six ending words in six different patterns of six-line stanzas (sestets), followed by a three-line envoi which uses all six of these refrained words. This gives the poem its 39 lines.

The sestina is a metered form, and as long as the pattern is maintained any meter may be employed; in the English language, iambic pentameter is the most common meter chosen.

The Pattern

If we look at the ending words for each line, and label them with the letters A to F, the first six-line stanza has the pattern:

A B C D E F

To generate the pattern for the second stanza, we take these letters and starting with the final one (F), we alternate picking up letters from the front and then the back until we have used all six. This gives us the following pattern for the second stanza:

F A E B D C

This diagram may better help to explain the pattern:

A B C D E F = F A E B D C

First Stanza   Second Stanza

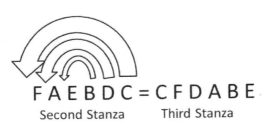

F A E B D C = C F D A B E

Second Stanza   Third Stanza

We repeat this same technique to create four more patterns, each one reordering the letters from the one above. Our resulting six stanza patterns look like this:

Stanza 1 – A B C D E F
Stanza 2 – F A E B D C
Stanza 3 – C F D A B E
Stanza 4 – E C B F A D
Stanza 5 – D E A C F B
Stanza 6 – B D F E C A

The final three-line envoi is done many ways. The only hard-and-fast rule here is that each line must end in one of the six words, and contain another inside, so that all six are used in these three lines. Purists will say that the pattern should be:

(B) E, (D) C, (A) F
Note: The parentheses mean that the word is used somewhere within the line.

This is how almost all sestinas were done during the height of their popularity. But since the 19th century, poets have made some changes, and now the most common patterns for the envoi lines are (A) B, (C) D, (E) F and (F) A, (E) B, (D) C.

The Circular Sestina

One of the changes that came about in the 19th century was the introduction of the circular, or rhyming, sestina. In order to make a rhyming pattern, two sets of three rhyming words are used: Lines A, C, and E rhyme, as do lines B, D, and F.

To accommodate the rhyming of these lines in alternating ABABAB and BABABA schemes, a new sestina pattern was created:

Stanza 1 – A B C D E F
Stanza 2 – F A D E B C
Stanza 3 – C F E B A D
Stanza 4 – D C B A F E
Stanza 5 – E D A F C B
Stanza 6 – B E F C D A
Envoi   – (A) F, (B) E, (C) D

An Example

The sestina has, since the resurgence of its popularity in the 1930s, become a vehicle more often used to produce lighthearted and humorous results. Puns have always been at home in the form, and sometimes the tales they tell are simple, yet strong:

Sestina

by Elizabeth Bishop (1911–1979)

September rain falls on the house.
In the failing light, the old grandmother
sits in the kitchen with the child
beside the Little Marvel Stove,
reading the jokes from the almanac,
laughing and talking to hide her tears.

She thinks that her equinoctial tears
and the rain that beats on the roof of the house
were both foretold by the almanac,
but only known to a grandmother.
The iron kettle sings on the stove.
She cuts some bread and says to the child,

It's time for tea now; but the child
is watching the teakettle's small hard tears
dance like mad on the hot black stove,
the way the rain must dance on the house.
Tidying up, the old grandmother
hangs up the clever almanac

on its string. Birdlike, the almanac
hovers half open above the child,
hovers above the old grandmother
and her teacup full of dark brown tears.
She shivers and says she thinks the house
feels chilly, and puts more wood in the stove.

It was to be, says the Marvel Stove.
I know what I know, says the almanac.
With crayons the child draws a rigid house
and a winding pathway. Then the child
puts in a man with buttons like tears
and shows it proudly to the grandmother.

But secretly, while the grandmother
busies herself about the stove,
the little moons fall down like tears
from between the pages of the almanac
into the flower bed the child
has carefully placed in the front of the house.

Time to plant tears, says the almanac.
The grandmother sings to the marvelous stove
and the child draws another inscrutable house.

This poem follows the classic sestina pattern, although the poet
chose to be a bit loose with the meter, and so the tale of the child and

grandmother becomes a bit less sober than it might have become had she stayed in metric form.

Crafting One of Your Own

The sestina is often used to tell a story, and that story can be in any genre. I have written westerns, romances, and even a comedy using the form, and while it is a challenge, like anything else it becomes easier as you practice. To craft a sestina, and indeed any structured form, I have a process, and that is what I would like to share with you.

The first step is to decide on your subject matter. My advice here is to begin with something or someone you know well.

For this example, I think I will create a story about my cousin. He is a homicide detective in a major metropolitan city, and he has been "on the job" for many years. I am not sure about the actual day-to-day life of a homicide detective, but like many others I read books and watch television shows and movies. This exposure to the make-believe world of crime fighting is all I really need to craft a fictionalized story, in verse.

Now comes the most important part in the creation of a sestina—the choice of your six repeating end words.

I get certain images in my mind when I picture a homicide detective. These initial mental images are, in my experience, the best things to use when crafting a narrative poem—regardless of the form. Therefore, I have chosen the following six words:

A = Job, B = Badge, C = Protect, D = Crime, E = Report, F = Night

Finally, before I can begin building the melodic lines in my poem, I must decide on a meter, so I can at least have a framework to craft upon. I have decided to use an 11-syllable meter, known as amphibrachic tetrameter catalectic. If this meter is unfamiliar, here is a syllabic representation of the rhythm, with "dee" being unstressed (soft) and "DUM" being stressed (hard) syllables:

<dee, DUM, dee> <dee, DUM, dee> <dee, DUM, dee> <dee, DUM>

So, with subject, words, and meter in hand, I can lay out the framework of the poem. Here is the first stanza, once the ending words are inserted. (The _ symbols signify soft syllables, and the = symbols are hard ones.)

(A) _ = _ _ = _ _ = _ _ job
(B) _ = _ _ = _ _ = _ _ badge
(C) _ = _ _ = _ _ = _ protect
(D) _ = _ _ = _ _ = _ _ crime
(E) _ = _ _ = _ _ = _ report
(F) _ = _ _ = _ _ = _ _ night

Now comes the fun part for the creative poet inside you. Using the rhythm of the meter, we tell our story, using the end words in the right places.

This is where your skill and dedication to painting word pictures comes into play, and it may take some time. If you write one stanza at a time, and then repeat the steps, you can create quite a compelling tale.

Using these steps, here is the completed poem I wrote, dedicated to my cousin, and all the men and women who put in long hours and energy bringing criminals to justice:

The Job

by Dusty Grein

It feels like forever I've been on the job.
Pinned down by the weight of my gun and my badge;
my duty is etched there, to serve and protect.
The uniforms tape off the scene of the crime
at this point, there still isn't much to report,
It promises to be one hell of a night.

My partner and I will work into the night;
It's on days like this I truly hate my job.
The worst part of all is the daily report,
Complete with the number and name from my badge
I lay out the facts of a hideous crime.
The victim is gone; one we failed to protect.

Now my reputation I have to protect.
From hero to scapegoat—it just takes one night;
a free-roaming villain, or one unsolved crime.
To close every case is the goal of the job,
the reason each day that I put on the badge.
I wish I could put that inside the report.

The televised anchors all love to report
to viewers—the public I've sworn to protect—
The slightest mistake by one who wears the badge.
The airwaves are filled with bad news every night,
I wish that good news was a part of their job
Like how, with hard work, we usually solve the crime.

I shudder recalling details from this crime;
gunfire—In my mind, I hear its report.
Deductive pretending is part of my job.
Sometimes sanity becomes hard to protect
when facing this ugliness night after night.
Emotions grow cold when you're wearing the badge.

My life? A lot simpler before the gold badge.
Back then it was mostly stopping petty crime,
And helping my neighbors sleep better at night.
I still had to fill out each detailed report,
the public I still did my best to protect;
promotions happen when you're good at your job.

"Now, wearing my badge is more than just a job,"
I repeat this each night as I write my report.
"By solving these crimes, my whole world I protect."

As you can see, the creation of a sestina is not as difficult as it may
seem going in. It does require the building of 39 metered lines, but
that is the job of a poet: to build word images and create emotional
and mental reactions through the creation of word art.

2.13 How to Write a Rhupunt (Welsh Form)

by Elizabeth Spencer Spragins

POETRY HAS BEEN an integral component of Welsh culture for centuries. Indeed, the Welsh word "bardd" (poet) has been traced back to 100 B.C. Depending on their skills, Welsh poets held one of three official ranks, and earning the designation of "chief poet" was a high honor. Every noble house in Wales boasted its own resident bard until the English legal system was imposed on the country in the 16th century. Although English law abolished the position of chief poet, the passion for poetry persisted.

Welsh poets demonstrated their skills through competitions with strict structural requirements. In the 14th century these poetic forms were codified into 24 official meters with three classes, one of which is the "awdl" (ode) meters, which includes the rhupunt.

The rhupunt (pronounced "hree-pint"), like other members of the awdl class, is stanzaic. Each stanza may have three, four, or five lines, and each line has four syllables. Within each stanza, all lines, with the exception of the last, share a single end rhyme. All of the last lines share a secondary end rhyme. Thus, a rhupunt with four-line stanzas would have the following rhyme scheme:

```
xxxa
xxxa
xxxa
xxxb

xxxc
xxxc
xxxc
xxxb

xxxd
xxxd
xxxd
xxxb
```

And so on.

In a variation known as the long rhupunt, each stanza is written as a single line, and the lines are paired in couplets. This format allows greater flexibility with the end rhyme, as illustrated below:

```
xxxaxxxaxxxaxxxb
xxxcxxxcxxxcxxxb

xxxdxxxdxxxdxxxe
xxxfxxxfxxxfxxxe
```

When written in the Welsh language, the awdl meters usually adhere to "cynhanedd" (rules of harmony governing consonance or alliteration). Although a rhupunt written in English does not necessarily follow this tradition, using such techniques to echo sounds within the lines can enhance the musicality of the poem.

My poem "Sedona" illustrates the structure of a rhupunt with four-line stanzas.

Sedona

by Elizabeth Spencer Spragins

Deep shadows fade
Red rock cascade
To purpled jade—
Sun sparks ignite.

Stone sentries stare
Sightless through air
At treadless stair
Spanning the height.

No mortals dare
Enter the lair
Or linger where
Spirit meets sprite.

This shrine of stone
And bleached white bone
Hides secrets shown
In the moonlight.

3. READING GREAT POETRY

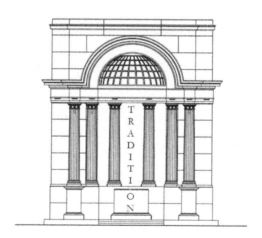

3.1 Ten of the Greatest Poems Ever Written

by Evan Mantyk

IN LEARNING TO write poetry, it is paramount to read great poetry. The 10 poems selected and presented here represent some of the greatest poems written originally in English and under 50 lines in length. At first, I compiled these under the title "Ten Best Poems Ever Written" and they appeared in the same order as they appear here, going from least greatest to greatest greatest. Of course, there is ample room to disagree on the order and the selected poems themselves. Nonetheless, what stands is that these 10 are definitely among the best left to us by history and have a wealth of poetic genius to share with us.

It is a good idea to read these poems aloud, read them frequently, and ideally memorize one or more of them.

For all of the poems, there are some basic questions that can be asked of students or of oneself. Analysis that I have provided after each poem illuminates the answers to some of these questions, but of course there is much more to be discovered and savored.

For Students

1. What new vocabulary words did you encounter? What are the definitions? Make sure that they match the context of the poem.

2. What is going on in this poem on the surface? Retell the poem in your own words, line-by-line.

3. What is the deeper meaning, or theme, of this poem?

4. What literary techniques—particularly, figurative language (similes, metaphors, personification), rhyme, meter, alliteration,

repetition, parallelism, symbolism, and imagery—is the poet using? What effect does the technique you point out have?

5. How does the historical period of the poet or biography of the poet increase our understanding of the poem? How does the poem increase our understanding of the historical period or poet's biography?

6. Why is this a great poem passed down for centuries?

7. Why is this poem still relevant today? Relate it to your own personal experiences or something else outside the poem.

8. What is the poet's perspective or view? Do you agree with it? Why or why not?

9. Write an introduction to the poem for someone who has never read it before.

10. Memorize one of the poems, dramatically recite it, and explain why you chose it.

The Road Not Taken

by Robert Frost (1874–1963)

Two roads diverged in a yellow wood,
And sorry I could not travel both
And be one traveler, long I stood
And looked down one as far as I could
To where it bent in the undergrowth;

Then took the other, as just as fair,
And having perhaps the better claim,
Because it was grassy and wanted wear;
Though as for that the passing there
Had worn them really about the same,

And both that morning equally lay
In leaves no step had trodden black.
Oh, I kept the first for another day!
Yet knowing how way leads on to way,
I doubted if I should ever come back.

I shall be telling this with a sigh
Somewhere ages and ages hence:
Two roads diverged in a wood, and I—
I took the one less traveled by,
And that has made all the difference.

Analysis of Poem 10: This poem deals with that big, noble question, "How to make a difference in the world?" On first reading, it tells us that the choice one makes really does matter, ending: "I took the one less traveled by, / And that has made all the difference."

A closer reading reveals that the lonely choice that was made earlier by our traveling narrator maybe wasn't all that significant since both roads were pretty much the same anyway ("Had worn them really about the same"), and it is only in the remembering and retelling that it made a difference. We are left to ponder if the narrator had instead traveled down "the road not taken," might it have also made a difference as well.

In a sense, "The Road Not Taken" tears apart the traditional view of individualism, which hinges on the importance of choice, as in the case of democracy in general (choosing a candidate), as well as various constitutional freedoms: choice of religion, choice of words (freedom of speech), choice of group (freedom of assembly), and choice of source of information (freedom of press). For example, we might imagine a young man choosing between being a carpenter or a banker later seeing great significance in his choice to be a banker, but in fact there was not much in his original decision at all other than a passing fancy. In this, we see the universality of human beings: the roads leading to carpenter and banker being basically the same, and the carpenter and banker at the end of them—seeming like individuals who made significant choices—really being just part of the collective of the human race.

Then is this poem not about the question of how to make a difference in the world, after all? No. It is still about this question. The ending is the clearest and most striking part. If nothing else, readers are left with the impression that our narrator, who commands beautiful verse, profound imagery, and time itself ("ages and ages hence"), puts value on striving to make a difference. The striving is reconstituted and complicated here in reflection, but our hero wants to make a difference and so should we. That is why this is a great poem, from a basic or close-reading perspective.

Robert Frost was a New England poet of the late Romantic and Modern periods. He spent his young adult years straddling both farming and teaching in rural New England. When he relocated his family to England to pursue poetry there, his career took off. They returned to New England after three years because of the outbreak of World War I, and he served in many eminent academic positions in the ensuing years.

The New Colossus

by Emma Lazarus (1849–1887)

Not like the brazen giant of Greek fame,
With conquering limbs astride from land to land;
Here at our sea-washed, sunset gates shall stand
A mighty woman with a torch, whose flame
Is the imprisoned lightning, and her name
Mother of Exiles. From her beacon-hand
Glows world-wide welcome; her mild eyes command
The air-bridged harbor that twin cities frame.

"Keep, ancient lands, your storied pomp!" cries she
With silent lips. "Give me your tired, your poor,
Your huddled masses yearning to breathe free,
The wretched refuse of your teeming shore.
Send these, the homeless, tempest-tossed to me,
I lift my lamp beside the golden door!"

Analysis of Poem 9

Inscribed on the Statue of Liberty in New York harbor, this sonnet may have the greatest placement of any English poem. It also has one of the greatest placements in history. Lazarus compares the Statue of Liberty to the Colossus of Rhodes, one of the Seven Wonders of the Ancient World. Like the Statue of Liberty, the Colossus of Rhodes was an enormous godlike statue positioned in a harbor. Although the Colossus of Rhodes no longer stands, it symbolizes the ancient Greek world and the greatness of the ancient Greek and Roman civilizations, which were lost for a thousand years to the West and only fully recovered during the Renaissance. "The New Colossus" succinctly crystallizes the connection between the ancient world and America, a modern nation. It's a connection that can be seen in the White House and other state and judicial buildings across America that architecturally mirror ancient Greek and Roman buildings, and in the American political system that mirrors Athenian Democracy and Roman Republicanism.

In the midst of this vast comparison of the ancient and the American, Lazarus still manages to clearly render America's distinct character. It is the can-do spirit of taking those persecuted and poor from around the world and giving them a new opportunity and hope for the future, what she calls "the golden door." It is a uniquely scrappy and compassionate quality that sets Americans apart from the ancients. The relevance of this poem stretches all the way back to the pilgrims fleeing religious persecution in Europe to the controversies surrounding modern immigrants from Mexico and the Middle East. While circumstances today have changed drastically, there is no denying that this open door was part of what made America great once upon a time. It's the perfect depiction of this quintessential Americanness that makes "The New Colossus" also outstanding.

Emma Lazarus was a New York poet of the Romantic period. Of aristocratic Jewish background, she worked for the defense of Judaism and Jews in Eastern Europe and throughout the world, as well as for the welfare of immigrants in the United States. Her poem "New Colossus" was at first forgotten among many poems written to help raise money for the building of the pedestal of the Statue of Liberty. After Lazarus's death, the poem was found by statue patron Georgina Schuyler, who selected it to be engraved on the statue. Indeed, the poem is a sort of Lazarus itself, Lazarus being a Biblical character raised from the dead.

Ozymandias

by Percy Bysshe Shelley (1792–1822)

I met a traveler from an antique land
Who said: "Two vast and trunkless legs of stone
Stand in the desert . . . Near them, on the sand,
Half sunk, a shattered visage lies, whose frown,
And wrinkled lip, and sneer of cold command,
Tell that its sculptor well those passions read
Which yet survive, stamped on these lifeless things,
The hand that mocked them, and the heart that fed:
And on the pedestal these words appear:
'My name is Ozymandias, king of kings:
Look on my works, ye Mighty, and despair!'
Nothing beside remains. Round the decay
Of that colossal wreck, boundless and bare
The lone and level sands stretch far away."

Analysis of Poem 8

In this winding story within a story within a poem, Shelley paints for us the image of the ruins of a statue of the ancient Egyptian king Ozymandias, who is today commonly known as Ramses II. This king is still regarded as the greatest and most powerful Egyptian pharaoh. Yet, all that's left of the statue are his legs, which tell us it was huge and impressive; the shattered head and snarling face, which tell us how tyrannical he was; and his inscribed quote hailing the magnificent structures that he built and that have been reduced to dust, which tells us they might not have been quite as magnificent as Ozymandias imagined. The image of a dictator-like king whose kingdom is no more creates a palpable irony. But beyond that, there is a perennial lesson about the inescapable and destructive forces of time, history, and nature—also called the transience, ephemeralness, mutability, or fleetingness of life. Success, fame, power, money, health, and prosperity can only last so long before fading into "lone and level sands."

There are yet more layers of meaning here that elevate this into one of the greatest poems. In terms of lost civilizations that show the ephemeralness of human pursuits, there is no better example than the Egyptians—whom we associate with such dazzling monuments as the Sphinx and the Great Pyramid at Giza (which stands far taller than the Statue of Liberty), yet who completely lost their spectacular language, culture, and civilization. If the forces of time, history, and nature can take down the Egyptian civilization, it begs the question "Who's next?" Additionally, Ozymandias is believed to have been the villainous pharaoh who enslaved the ancient Hebrews and from whom Moses led the exodus. If all ordinary pursuits, such as power and fame, are but dust, what remains, the poem suggests, are spirituality and morality—embodied by the ancient Hebrew faith. If you don't have those, then in the long run you are a "colossal wreck." Thus, the perfectly composed scene itself, the Egyptian imagery, and the Biblical backstory convey a perennial message that makes this a great poem.

Percy Bysshe Shelley was an English poet of the Romantic period. Coming from an aristocratic background, he is known for his freewheeling idealism. He broke social and political norms of the time, including marrying below his class, remarrying, opposing monarchy, and opposing organized religion. At the age of 30, while living in Italy, he and a friend died when a storm sank their boat.

Ode on a Grecian Urn

by John Keats (1795–1821)

Thou still unravish'd bride of quietness,
   Thou foster-child of silence and slow time,
Sylvan historian, who canst thus express
   A flowery tale more sweetly than our rhyme:
What leaf-fring'd legend haunts about thy shape
   Of deities or mortals, or of both,
      In Tempe or the dales of Arcady?
     What men or gods are these? What maidens loth?
What mad pursuit? What struggle to escape?
     What pipes and timbrels? What wild ecstasy?

Heard melodies are sweet, but those unheard
   Are sweeter; therefore, ye soft pipes, play on;
Not to the sensual ear, but, more endear'd,
   Pipe to the spirit ditties of no tone:
Fair youth, beneath the trees, thou canst not leave
   Thy song, nor ever can those trees be bare;
     Bold Lover, never, never canst thou kiss,
     Though winning near the goal yet, do not grieve;
She cannot fade, though thou hast not thy bliss,
     For ever wilt thou love, and she be fair!

Ah, happy, happy boughs! that cannot shed
   Your leaves, nor ever bid the Spring adieu;
And, happy melodist, unwearied,
   For ever piping songs for ever new;
More happy love! more happy, happy love!
   For ever warm and still to be enjoy'd,
     For ever panting, and for ever young;
   All breathing human passion far above,
That leaves a heart high-sorrowful and cloy'd,
     A burning forehead, and a parching tongue.

Who are these coming to the sacrifice?
   To what green altar, O mysterious priest,
Lead'st thou that heifer lowing at the skies,
   And all her silken flanks with garlands drest?

What little town by river or sea shore,
　　Or mountain-built with peaceful citadel,
　　　Is emptied of this folk, this pious morn?
　　And, little town, thy streets for evermore
Will silent be; and not a soul to tell
　　　Why thou art desolate, can e'er return.

O Attic shape! Fair attitude! with brede
　　Of marble men and maidens overwrought,
With forest branches and the trodden weed;
　　Thou, silent form, dost tease us out of thought
As doth eternity: Cold Pastoral!
　　When old age shall this generation waste,
　　　Thou shalt remain, in midst of other woe
　　Than ours, a friend to man, to whom thou say'st,
"Beauty is truth, truth beauty,—that is all
　　　Ye know on earth, and all ye need to know."

Analysis of Poem 7

As if in response to Shelley's "Ozymandias," Keats's "Ode on a Grecian Urn" offers a sort of antidote to the inescapable and destructive force of time. Indeed, "Ode on a Grecian Urn" was published in 1819, just a year or so after "Ozymandias." The antidote is simple: art. The art on the Grecian urn—which is basically a decorative pot from ancient Greece—has survived for thousands of years. While empires rose and fell, the Grecian urn survived. Musicians, trees, lovers, heifers, and priests all continue dying decade after decade and century after century, but their artistic depictions on the Grecian urn live on for what seems eternity.

This realization about the timeless nature of art is not new now, nor was it in the 1800s, but Keats has chosen a perfect example since ancient Greek civilization so famously disappeared into the ages, being subsumed by the Romans, and mostly lost until the Renaissance a thousand years later. Now, the ancient Greeks are all certainly dead (like the king Ozymandias in Shelley's poem), but the Greek art and culture live on—through Renaissance painters, the Olympic Games, endemic Neoclassical architecture, and, of course, the Grecian urn.

Further, what is depicted on the Grecian urn is a variety of life that makes the otherwise cold urn feel alive and vibrant. This aliveness is accentuated by Keats's barrage of questions and blaring exclamations: "More happy love! more happy, happy love!" Art, he seems to suggest, is more alive and real than we might imagine. Indeed, the last two lines can be read as the urn itself talking: "Beauty is truth, truth beauty,—that is all / Ye know on earth, and all ye need to know." In these profound lines, Keats places us within ignorance, suggesting that what we know on earth is limited, but that artistic beauty, which he has now established is alive, is connected with truth. Thus, we can escape ignorance, humanness, and certain death and approach another form of life, approach the truth, through the beauty of art. This effectively completes the thought that began in "Ozymandias" and makes this a great poem one notch up from its predecessor.

John Keats was an English poet of the Romantic period. From relatively humble origins as the son of a horse-stable owner to a job as an apprentice surgeon, Keats rose to become a poet of moderate significance in his time, but he died at just 26 from tuberculosis. Posthumously, his poetry, known for its imagery and passion, has been greatly celebrated.

The Tiger

by William Blake (1757–1827)

Tiger Tiger, burning bright,
In the forests of the night;
What immortal hand or eye,
Could frame thy fearful symmetry?

In what distant deeps or skies.
Burnt the fire of thine eyes?
On what wings dare he aspire?
What the hand, dare seize the fire?

And what shoulder, and what art,
Could twist the sinews of thy heart?
And when thy heart began to beat,
What dread hand? and what dread feet?

What the hammer? what the chain,
In what furnace was thy brain?
What the anvil? what dread grasp,
Dare its deadly terrors clasp!

When the stars threw down their spears
And water'd heaven with their tears:
Did he smile his work to see?
Did he who made the Lamb make thee?

Tiger Tiger burning bright,
In the forests of the night:
What immortal hand or eye,
Dare frame thy fearful symmetry?

Analysis of Poem 6: This poem contemplates a question arising from the belief in creation by an intelligent creator. The question is this: If there is a loving, compassionate God or gods who created human beings and whose great powers exceed the comprehension of human beings, as many major religions hold, then why would such a powerful being allow evil into the world? Evil here is represented by a tiger that might, should you be strolling in the Indian or African wild in the 1700s, have leapt out and killed you. What would have created such a dangerous and evil creature? How could it possibly be the same divine blacksmith who created a cute, harmless, fluffy lamb or who created Jesus, also known as the "Lamb of God" (which the devoutly Christian Blake was probably also referring to here)? To put it another way, why would such a divine blacksmith create beautiful, innocent children and then also allow such children to be slaughtered? The battery of questions brings this mystery to life with lavish intensity.

Does Blake offer an answer to this question of evil from a good God? It would seem not on the surface. But this wouldn't be a great poem if it were really that open-ended. The answer comes in the way that Blake explains the question. Blake's language peels away the mundane world and offers a look at the super-reality that poets are privy to. We fly about in "forests of the night" through "distant deeps or skies," looking for where the fire in the tiger's eye was taken from by the Creator. This is the reality of expanded time, space, and perception that Blake so clearly elucidates elsewhere with the lines, "To see a world in a grain of sand / And a heaven in a wild flower, / Hold infinity in the palm of your hand, / And eternity in an hour." (from "Auguries of Innocence"). This indirectly tells us that the reality we ordinarily know and perceive is really insufficient, shallow, and deceptive. Where we perceive the injustice of the wild tiger, something else entirely may be transpiring. What we ordinarily take for truth may really be far from it: a thought that is scary, yet also sublime or beautiful—like the beautiful and fearsome tiger. Thus, this poem is great because it concisely and compellingly presents a question that still plagues humanity today, as well as a key clue to the answer.

William Blake was an English poet of the Renaissance and early Romantic periods. He was also a skilled engraver and artist. Although against organized religion, he was passionately Christian and frequently had visions throughout his life.

On His Blindness

by John Milton (1608–1674)

When I consider how my light is spent
 Ere half my days in this dark world and wide,
 And that one talent which is death to hide
 Lodg'd with me useless, though my soul more bent
To serve therewith my Maker, and present
 My true account, lest he returning chide,
 "Doth God exact day-labour, light denied?"
 I fondly ask. But Patience, to prevent
That murmur, soon replies: "God doth not need
 Either man's work or his own gifts: who best
 Bear his mild yoke, they serve him best. His state
Is kingly; thousands at his bidding speed
 And post o'er land and ocean without rest:
 They also serve who only stand and wait."

Analysis of Poem 5

This poem deals with one's limitations and shortcomings in life. Everyone has them, and Milton's blindness is a perfect example of this. His eyesight gradually worsened, and he became totally blind at the age of 42. This happened after he served in an eminent position under Oliver Cromwell's Puritan government in England. To put it simply, Milton rose to the highest position an English writer might at the time and then sank all the way down to a state of being unable to read or write on his own. How pathetic!

The genius of this poem comes in the way that Milton transcends the misery he feels. First, he frames himself, not as an individual suffering or lonely, but as a failed servant to the Creator: God. While Milton is disabled, God here is enabled through imagery of a king commanding thousands. This celestial monarch, his ministers and troops, and his kingdom itself are invisible to human eyes anyway, so already Milton has subtly undone much of his failing by subverting the necessity for human vision. More straightforwardly, through the voice of Patience, Milton explains that serving the celestial monarch only requires bearing those hardships, which really aren't that bad (he calls them "mild"), that life has burdened you with (like a "yoke" put on an ox). This grand mission from heaven may be as simple as standing and waiting, having patience, and understanding the order of the universe. Thus, this is a great poem because Milton has not only dispelled sadness over a major shortcoming in life but also shown how the shortcoming is itself imbued with an extraordinary and uplifting purpose.

John Milton was an English poet of the late Renaissance period. He is most noted for his epic poem on the fall of Satan and Adam and Eve's ejection from the Garden of Eden, *Paradise Lost,* which he composed after having gone blind. During his time, he was known for his strong Puritan faith, opposition to the Church of England and the pope, and his support for personal freedoms. After the English Civil War and the ascension of the Puritan general and parliamentarian Oliver Cromwell over the Commonwealth of England, Milton was given a high position, making him essentially head propagandist.

A Psalm of Life
What the heart of the young man said to the Psalmist

by Henry Wadsworth Longfellow (1807–1882)

Tell me not, in mournful numbers,
  Life is but an empty dream!
For the soul is dead that slumbers,
  And things are not what they seem.

Life is real! Life is earnest!
  And the grave is not its goal;
Dust thou art, to dust returnest,
  Was not spoken of the soul.

Not enjoyment, and not sorrow,
  Is our destined end or way;
But to act, that each tomorrow
  Find us farther than today.

Art is long, and Time is fleeting,
  And our hearts, though stout and brave,
Still, like muffled drums, are beating
  Funeral marches to the grave.

In the world's broad field of battle,
  In the bivouac of Life,
Be not like dumb, driven cattle!
  Be a hero in the strife!

Trust no Future, howe'er pleasant!
  Let the dead Past bury its dead!
Act,—act in the living Present!
  Heart within, and God o'erhead!

Lives of great men all remind us
  We can make our lives sublime,
And, departing, leave behind us
  Footprints on the sands of time;—

Footprints, that perhaps another,
    Sailing o'er life's solemn main,
A forlorn and shipwrecked brother,
    Seeing, shall take heart again.

Let us, then, be up and doing,
    With a heart for any fate;
Still achieving, still pursuing,
    Learn to labor and to wait.

Analysis of Poem 4

In this nine-stanza poem, the first six stanzas are rather vague since each stanza seems to begin a new thought. Instead, the emphasis here is on a feeling rather than a rational train of thought. What feeling? It seems to be a reaction against science, which is focused on calculations ("mournful numbers") and empirical evidence, of which there is none, or very little, to prove the existence of the soul. Longfellow lived when the Industrial Revolution was in high gear and the ideals of science, rationality, and reason flourished. From this perspective, the fact that the first six stanzas do not follow a rational train of thought makes perfect sense.

According to the poem, the force of science seems to restrain one's spirit or soul ("For the soul is dead that slumbers"), leading to inaction and complacency from which we must break free ("Act,— act in the living Present! / Heart within, and God o'erhead!") for lofty purposes such as Art, Heart, and God before time runs out ("Art is long, and Time is fleeting"). The last three stanzas—which, having broken free from science by this point in the poem, read more smoothly—suggest that this acting for lofty purposes can lead to greatness and can help our fellow man.

We might think of the entire poem as a clarion call to do great things, however insignificant they may seem in the present and on the empirically observable surface. That may mean writing a poem and entering it into a poetry contest, when you know the chances of your poem winning are very small; risking your life for something you believe in, when you know it is not popular or it is misunderstood; or volunteering for a cause that, although it may seem hopeless, you feel is truly important. Thus, the greatness of this poem lies in its ability to so clearly prescribe a method for greatness in our modern world.

Henry Wadsworth Longfellow was an American poet of the Romantic period. He served as a professor at Harvard and was an adept linguist, traveling throughout Europe and immersing himself in European culture and poetry, which he emulated in his poetry. Before television, radio, and film, he rose to become not just the leading poet and literary figure of 19th-century America, but also an American icon and household name.

Daffodils

by William Wordsworth (1770–1850)

I wandered lonely as a cloud
   That floats on high o'er vales and hills,
When all at once I saw a crowd,
   A host, of golden daffodils;
Beside the lake, beneath the trees,
Fluttering and dancing in the breeze.

Continuous as the stars that shine
   And twinkle on the milky way,
They stretched in never-ending line
   Along the margin of a bay:
Ten thousand saw I at a glance,
Tossing their heads in sprightly dance.

The waves beside them danced; but they
   Out-did the sparkling waves in glee:
A poet could not but be gay,
   In such a jocund company:
I gazed—and gazed—but little thought
What wealth the show to me had brought:

For oft, when on my couch I lie
   In vacant or in pensive mood,
They flash upon that inward eye
   Which is the bliss of solitude;
And then my heart with pleasure fills,
And dances with the daffodils.

Analysis of Poem 3

Through the narrator's chance encounter with a field of daffodils by the water, we are presented with the power and beauty of the natural world. It sounds simple enough, but there are several factors that contribute to this poem's greatness. First, the poem comes at a time when the Western world is industrializing and man feels spiritually lonely in the face of an increasingly godless worldview. This feeling is perfectly harnessed by the depiction of wandering through the wilderness "lonely as a cloud" and by the ending scene of the narrator sadly lying on his couch "in vacant or in pensive mood" and finding happiness in solitude. The daffodils then become more than nature; they become a companion and a source of personal joy.

Second, the very simplicity itself of enjoying nature—flowers, trees, the sea, the sky, the mountains, and so on—is perfectly manifested by the simplicity of the poem: The four stanzas simply begin with daffodils, describe daffodils, compare daffodils to something else, and end on daffodils, respectively. Any common reader can easily get this poem, as easily as he or she might enjoy a walk around a lake.

Third, Wordsworth has subtly put forward more than just an ode to nature here. Every stanza mentions dancing, and the third stanza even calls the daffodils "a show." At this time in England, one might have paid money to see an opera or other performance of high quality. Here, Wordsworth is putting forward the idea that nature can offer similar joys and even give you "wealth" instead of taking it from you, undoing the idea that beauty is attached to earthly money and social status. This, coupled with the language and topic of the poem, which are both relatively accessible to the common man, makes for a great poem that demonstrates the all-encompassing and accessible nature of beauty and its associates: truth and bliss.

William Wordsworth was an English poet who was a seminal figure of the Romantic period. Along with Samuel Taylor Coleridge, Wordsworth published a collection of short poems, titled *Lyrical Ballads,* addressing often common experiences with common language, effectively breaking from the Neoclassical style that dominated at the time. He rose to the post of Poet Laureate of England.

Holy Sonnet 10:
Death, Be Not Proud

by John Donne (1572–1631)

Death, be not proud, though some have called thee
Mighty and dreadful, for thou art not so;
For those whom thou think'st thou dost overthrow
Die not, poor Death, nor yet canst thou kill me.
From rest and sleep, which but thy pictures be,
Much pleasure; then from thee much more must flow,
And soonest our best men with thee do go,
Rest of their bones, and soul's delivery.
Thou art slave to fate, chance, kings, and desperate men,
And dost with poison, war, and sickness dwell,
And poppy or charms can make us sleep as well
And better than thy stroke; why swell'st thou then?
One short sleep past, we wake eternally
And death shall be no more; Death, thou shalt die.

Analysis of Poem 2: Death is a perennial subject of fear and despair. But this sonnet seems to say that it need not be this way. The highly focused attack on Death's sense of pride uses a grocery list of rhetorical attacks: First, sleep, which is the closest human experience to death, is actually quite nice. Second, all great people die sooner or later, and the process of death could be viewed as joining them. Third, Death is under the command of higher authorities such as fate, which controls accidents, and kings, who wage wars. From this perspective, Death seems no more than a pawn in a larger chess game within the universe. Fourth, Death must associate with some unsavory characters: "poison, wars, and sickness." Yikes! They must make unpleasant coworkers! (You can almost see Donne laughing as he wrote this.) Fifth, "poppy and charms" (drugs) can do the sleep job as well as Death or better.

The sixth, most compelling, and most serious reason is that if one truly believes in a soul then Death is really nothing to worry about. The soul lives eternally and this explains line 4, when Donne says that Death can't kill him. If you recognize the subordinate position of the body in the universe and identify more fully with your soul, then you can't be killed in an ordinary sense.

Further, this poem is so great because of its universal application. Fear of death is so natural an instinct and Death itself so all-encompassing and inescapable for people, that the spirit of this poem and applicability of it extends to almost any fear or weakness of character that one might have. Confronting, head on, such a fear or weakness, as Donne has done here, allows human beings to transcend their condition and their perception of Death, more fully perhaps than one might through art by itself—as many poets in this list seem to say—since the art may or may not survive, may or may not be any good, but the intrinsic quality of one's soul lives eternally. Thus, Donne leaves a powerful lesson: Confront what you fear head on and remember that there is nothing to fear on earth if you believe in a soul.

John Donne was a major English poet of the late Renaissance period. While serving as secretary for the Duke of Egerton, he married the Duke's niece secretly and, as a consequence, was briefly imprisoned. He was no longer viewed suitable for public service and spent the next period of his life relatively impoverished. During this period, the couple had many children, while Donne produced many literary works for various patrons. Late in his life, he became a devoted cleric in the Church of England.

Sonnet 18

by William Shakespeare (1564–1616)

Shall I compare thee to a summer's day?
Thou art more lovely and more temperate:
Rough winds do shake the darling buds of May,
And summer's lease hath all too short a date:
Sometime too hot the eye of heaven shines,
And often is his gold complexion dimm'd;
And every fair from fair sometime declines,
By chance, or nature's changing course, untrimm'd;
But thy eternal summer shall not fade
Nor lose possession of that fair thou ow'st;
Nor shall Death brag thou wander'st in his shade,
When in eternal lines to time thou grow'st;
    So long as men can breathe or eyes can see,
    So long lives this, and this gives life to thee.

Analysis of Poem 1

In this poem, the narrator tells someone whom he esteems highly that this person is better than a summer's day because a summer's day is often too hot and too windy, and especially because a summer's day doesn't last. It must fade away just as people, plants, and animals die—again, the fleeting nature of life. But this esteemed person does not lose beauty or fade away like a summer's day because he or she is eternally preserved in the narrator's own poetry. "So long lives this, and this gives life to thee" means "This poetry lives long, and this poetry gives life to you."

From a modern perspective, this poem might come off as pompous (assuming the greatness of one's own poetry), arbitrary (criticizing a summer's day upon what seems a whim), and sycophantic (praising someone without substantial evidence). How then could this possibly be number one? After the bad taste of an old flavor to a modern tongue wears off, we realize that this is the very best of poetry. This is not pompous because Shakespeare actually achieves greatness and creates an eternal poem. It is okay to recognize poetry as great if it is great, and it is okay to recognize an artistic hierarchy. In fact, it is absolutely necessary in educating, guiding, and leading others.

The attack on a summer's day is not arbitrary. Woven throughout the language is an implicit and profound connection between human beings, the natural world ("a summer's day"), and heaven (the sun is "the eye of heaven"). The comparison of a human being to a summer's day immediately opens the mind to unconventional possibilities, to spiritual perspectives, to the ethereal realm of poetry and beauty.

The unabashed praise for someone without a hint as to even the gender or accomplishments of the person is not irrational or sycophantic. It is a pure and simple way of approaching our relationships with other people, assuming the best. It is a happier way to live—immediately free from the depression, stress, and cynicism that creeps into our hearts. Thus, this poem is strikingly and refreshingly bold, profound, and uplifting.

Finally, as to the question of the fleeting nature of life, an overarching theme in these great poems, Shakespeare adroitly answers it by skipping the question, suggesting it is of no consequence. He wields such sublime power that he is unmoved and can instead offer remedy, his verse, at will to those he sees befitting and may themselves harbor such worries. How marvelous!

William Shakespeare, also known simply as the Bard, was an English poet and playwright of the Renaissance period. Although he is probably the most significant figure in all of English literature, Shakespeare's history remains debated. Many scholars and much research suggest his plays were really written by the Earl of Oxford, Edward de Vere, a courtier in Queen Elizabeth I's court who could not openly associate himself with the low culture of theater. At any rate, Shakespeare's work include a long list of acclaimed plays, such as *Hamlet, Julius Caesar, Henry V, Merchant of Venice, Romeo and Juliet,* and *A Midsummer Night's Dream,* to name only a few, Shakespeare is frequently cited for his beautiful language (often in verse form) and his ability to stirringly portray the human experience through his multifaceted characters, universal themes, and brilliant storylines.

3.2 Nine Love Poems

by Conrad Geller

THE POEMS I have chosen cover the full spectrum of responses to love, from joy to anguish, and sometimes a mixture of both. As befits the topic, the list is a bit heavy on Romantics and light on those rational Enlightenment types. Here, with a few comments and no apologies, is the list:

Love Poem 9

It may be a bad augury to begin with a poem by a loser, but there it is. Michael Drayton, a contemporary and possible acquaintance of the Bard, evidently had come to the unhappy end of an affair when he penned this sonnet. He begins with a show of stoic indifference: "... you get no more of me," but that can't last. In the last six lines, he shows his true feelings with a series of personifications of the dying figures of Love, Passion, Faith, and Innocence, which he pleads can be saved from their fate by the lady's kindness.

Since There's No Help

by Michael Drayton (1563–1631)

Since there's no help, come let us kiss and part;
Nay, I have done, you get no more of me,
And I am glad, yea glad with all my heart
That thus so cleanly I myself can free;
Shake hands forever, cancel all our vows,
And when we meet at any time again,
Be it not seen in either of our brows
That we one jot of former love retain.
Now at the last gasp of Love's latest breath,
When, his pulse failing, Passion speechless lies,
When Faith is kneeling by his bed of death,
And Innocence is closing up his eyes,
 Now if thou wouldst, when all have given him over,
 From death to life thou mightst him yet recover.

Love Poem 8

If poetry, as Wordsworth asserted, is "emotion recollected in tranquility," this sonnet scores high in the former essential but falls short of the latter. Elizabeth may have been the original arts groupie, whose passion for the famous poet Robert Browning seems to have known no limits and recognized no excesses. She loves she says "with my childhood's faith," her beloved now holding the place of her "lost saints." No wonder this poem, whatever its hyperbole, has long been a favorite of adolescent girls and matrons who remember what it was like.

How Do I Love Thee

by Elizabeth Barrett Browning (1806–1861)

How do I love thee? Let me count the ways.
I love thee to the depth and breadth and height
My soul can reach, when feeling out of sight
For the ends of being and ideal grace.
I love thee to the level of every day's
Most quiet need, by sun and candle-light.
I love thee freely, as men strive for right.
I love thee purely, as they turn from praise.
I love thee with the passion put to use
In my old griefs, and with my childhood's faith.
I love thee with a love I seemed to lose
With my lost saints. I love thee with the breath,
Smiles, tears, of all my life; and, if God choose,
I shall but love thee better after death.

Love Poem 7

Here we have a bold attempt at seduction, this one much longer and more complicated than Shelley's "Love's Philosophy" (see page 18). In this poem, the lover is attempting to gain his desire by appealing to the tender emotions of his object. He sings her a song about the days of chivalry, in which a knight saved a lady from an "outrage worst than death" (whatever that is), is wounded, and eventually dies in her arms. The poet's beloved, on hearing the story, is deeply moved to tears and, to make the story not as long as the original, succumbs.

As with his most famous poem, "The Rime of the Ancient Mariner," Coleridge employs the oldest of English forms, the ballad stanza, but here he uses a lengthened second line. Coleridge, by the way, could really tell a romantic story, whatever his ulterior motives.

Love

by Samuel Taylor Coleridge (1772–1834)

All thoughts, all passions, all delights,
Whatever stirs this mortal frame,
All are but ministers of Love,
And feed his sacred flame.

Oft in my waking dreams do I
Live o'er again that happy hour,
When midway on the mount I lay,
Beside the ruined tower.

The moonshine, stealing o'er the scene
Had blended with the lights of eve;
And she was there, my hope, my joy,
My own dear Genevieve!

She leant against the arméd man,
The statue of the arméd knight;
She stood and listened to my lay,
Amid the lingering light.

Few sorrows hath she of her own,
My hope! my joy! my Genevieve!

She loves me best, whene'er I sing
The songs that make her grieve.

I played a soft and doleful air,
I sang an old and moving story—
An old rude song, that suited well
That ruin wild and hoary.

She listened with a flitting blush,
With downcast eyes and modest grace;
For well she knew, I could not choose
But gaze upon her face.

I told her of the Knight that wore
Upon his shield a burning brand;
And that for ten long years he wooed
The Lady of the Land.

I told her how he pined: and ah!
The deep, the low, the pleading tone
With which I sang another's love,
Interpreted my own.

She listened with a flitting blush,
With downcast eyes, and modest grace;
And she forgave me, that I gazed
Too fondly on her face!

But when I told the cruel scorn
That crazed that bold and lovely Knight,
And that he crossed the mountain-woods,
Nor rested day nor night;

That sometimes from the savage den,
And sometimes from the darksome shade,
And sometimes starting up at once
In green and sunny glade,—

There came and looked him in the face
An angel beautiful and bright;

And that he knew it was a Fiend,
This miserable Knight!

And that unknowing what he did,
He leaped amid a murderous band,
And saved from outrage worse than death
The Lady of the Land!

And how she wept, and clasped his knees;
And how she tended him in vain—
And ever strove to expiate
The scorn that crazed his brain;—

And that she nursed him in a cave;
And how his madness went away,
When on the yellow forest-leaves
A dying man he lay;—
His dying words—but when I reached
That tenderest strain of all the ditty,
My faultering voice and pausing harp
Disturbed her soul with pity!

All impulses of soul and sense
Had thrilled my guileless Genevieve;
The music and the doleful tale,
The rich and balmy eve;

And hopes, and fears that kindle hope,
An undistinguishable throng,
And gentle wishes long subdued,
Subdued and cherished long!

She wept with pity and delight,
She blushed with love, and virgin-shame;
And like the murmur of a dream,
I heard her breathe my name.

Her bosom heaved—she stepped aside,
As conscious of my look she stepped—
Then suddenly, with timorous eye
She fled to me and wept.

She half enclosed me with her arms,
She pressed me with a meek embrace;
And bending back her head, looked up,
And gazed upon my face.

'Twas partly love, and partly fear,
And partly 'twas a bashful art,
That I might rather feel, than see,
The swelling of her heart.

I calmed her fears, and she was calm,
And told her love with virgin pride;
And so I won my Genevieve,
My bright and beauteous Bride.

Love Poem 6

Burns's best-known poem besides "Auld Lang Syne" is a simple declaration of feeling. "How beautiful and delightful is my love," he says. "You are so lovely, in fact, that I will love you to the end of time. And even though we are parting now, I will return, no matter what." All this is expressed in a breathtaking excess of metaphor: "And I will love thee still, my dear, / Till a' the seas gang dry." This poem has no peer as a simple cry of a young man who knows no boundaries.

A Red, Red Rose

by Robert Burns (1759–1796)

O my Luve is like a red, red rose
That's newly sprung in June;
O my Luve is like the melody
That's sweetly played in tune.

So fair art thou, my bonnie lass,
So deep in luve am I;
And I will luve thee still, my dear,
Till a' the seas gang dry.

Till a' the seas gang dry, my dear,
And the rocks melt wi' the sun;
I will love thee still, my dear,
While the sands o' life shall run.

And fare thee weel, my only luve!
And fare thee weel awhile!
And I will come again, my luve,
Though it were ten thousand mile.

Love Poem 5

Poe shows off his amazing talent in the manipulation of language sounds here, perhaps his best-known poem after "The Raven." It's a festival of auditory effects, with a delightful mixture of anapests and iambs, internal rhymes, repetitions, and assonances. The story itself is a Poe favorite, the tragic death of a beautiful, loved girl, who died after her "high-born kinsman" separated her from the lover.

Annabel Lee

by Edgar Allan Poe (1809–1849)

It was many and many a year ago,
In a kingdom by the sea,
That a maiden there lived whom you may know
By the name of Annabel Lee;
And this maiden she lived with no other thought
Than to love and be loved by me.

I was a child and she was a child,
In this kingdom by the sea:
But we loved with a love that was more than love—
I and my Annabel Lee;
With a love that the wingéd seraphs of heaven
Laughed loud at her and me.

And this was the reason that, long ago,
In this kingdom by the sea,
A wind blew out of a cloud, chilling
My beautiful Annabel Lee;
So that her highborn kinsman came
And bore her away from me,
To shut her up in a sepulchre
In this kingdom by the sea.

The angels, not half so happy in heaven,
Went laughing at her and me—
Yes!—that was the reason (as all men know,
In this kingdom by the sea)

That the wind came out of the cloud by night,
Chilling and killing my Annabel Lee.

But our love it was stronger by far than the love
Of those who were older than we—
Of many far wiser than we—
And neither the laughter in heaven above,
Nor the demons down under the sea,
Can ever dissever my soul from the soul
Of the beautiful Annabel Lee:

For the moon never beams, without bringing me dreams
Of the beautiful Annabel Lee;
And the stars never rise, but I feel the bright eyes
Of the beautiful Annabel Lee;
And so, all the night-tide, I lie down by the side
Of my darling—my darling—my life and my bride,
In her sepulchre there by the sea,
In her tomb by the sounding sea.

Love Poem 4

Supposedly written about Anne Boleyn, wife of King Henry VIII, this bitter poem compares Wyatt's beloved to a deer fleeing before an exhausted hunter, who finally gives up the chase because, as he says, "in a net I seek to hold the wind." Besides, he reflects, she is the king's property, and forbidden anyway. The bitterness comes mainly in the first line: "I know where there is a female deer, if anyone wants to go after her." As the history goes, she could not produce the male heir Henry wanted and he (probably) wrongfully accused her of incest and adultery just so he could have her executed. This love, hijacked by higher forces, painfully elusive, and wildly tempting, is exquisitely real and compelling.

Whoso List to Hunt

by Sir Thomas Wyatt (1503–1542)

Whoso list to hunt, I know where is an hind,
But as for me, alas, I may no more.
The vain travail hath wearied me so sore,
I am of them that farthest cometh behind.
Yet may I by no means my wearied mind
Draw from the deer, but as she fleeth afore
Fainting I follow. I leave off therefore,
Since in a net I seek to hold the wind.
Who list her hunt, I put him out of doubt,
As well as I may spend his time in vain.
And graven with diamonds in letters plain
There is written, her fair neck round about:
"Noli me tangere, for Caesar's I am,
And wild for to hold, though I seem tame."

Whoso list: whoever wants
Hind: Female deer
Noli me tangere: "Don't touch me"

Love Poem 3

Yet another seduction attempt in verse, perhaps this poem doesn't belong on a list like this, since it isn't about love at all. The lover is trying to convince a reluctant ('coy") lady to accede to his importuning, not by a sad story, as in the Coleridge poem, or by an appeal to nature, as in Shelley, but by a formal argument: Sexuality ends with death, which is inevitable, so what are you saving it for?

> ... then worms shall try
> That long preserved virginity,
> And your quaint honour turn to dust,
> And into ashes all my lust.

And it ends with the pointed suggestion,

> Let us roll all our strength and all
> Our sweetness up into one ball,
> And tear our pleasures with rough strife
> Thorough the iron gates of life.

This is one of the best poems in the English language, so I'll include it here, whether it can be strictly pinned down with a label like love or death or not.

To His Coy Mistress

by Andrew Marvell (1621–1678)

> Had we but world enough and time,
> This coyness, lady, were no crime.
> We would sit down, and think which way
> To walk, and pass our long love's day.
> Thou by the Indian Ganges' side
> Shouldst rubies find; I by the tide
> Of Humber would complain. I would
> Love you ten years before the flood,
> And you should, if you please, refuse
> Till the conversion of the Jews.
> My vegetable love should grow
> Vaster than empires and more slow;
> An hundred years should go to praise

Thine eyes, and on thy forehead gaze;
Two hundred to adore each breast,
But thirty thousand to the rest;
An age at least to every part,
And the last age should show your heart.
For, lady, you deserve this state,
Nor would I love at lower rate.

But at my back I always hear
Time's wingèd chariot hurrying near;
And yonder all before us lie
Deserts of vast eternity.
Thy beauty shall no more be found;
Nor, in thy marble vault, shall sound
My echoing song; then worms shall try
That long-preserved virginity,
And your quaint honour turn to dust,
And into ashes all my lust;
The grave's a fine and private place,
But none, I think, do there embrace.

Now therefore, while the youthful hue
Sits on thy skin like morning dew,
And while thy willing soul transpires
At every pore with instant fires,
Now let us sport us while we may,
And now, like amorous birds of prey,
Rather at once our time devour
Than languish in his slow-chapped power.
Let us roll all our strength and all
Our sweetness up into one ball,
And tear our pleasures with rough strife
Through the iron gates of life:
Thus, though we cannot make our sun
Stand still, yet we will make him run.

Love Poem 2

Keats brings an almost overwhelming sensuality to this sonnet. Surprisingly, the first eight lines are not about love or even human life; Keats looks at a personified star. (Venus? But it's not steadfast. The North Star? It's steadfast but not particularly bright.) Whatever star it may be, the sestet finds the lover "Pillow'd upon my fair love's ripening breast," where he plans to stay forever, or at least until death. Somehow, the surprising juxtaposition of the wide view of the earth as seen from the heavens and the intimate picture of the lovers works to invest the scene of dalliance with a cosmic importance. John Donne sometimes accomplished this same effect, though none of his poems made my final cut.

Bright Star

by John Keats (1795–1821)

Bright star, would I were stedfast as thou art—
Not in lone splendour hung aloft the night
And watching, with eternal lids apart,
Like nature's patient, sleepless Eremite,
The moving waters at their priestlike task
Of pure ablution round earth's human shores,
Or gazing on the new soft-fallen mask
Of snow upon the mountains and the moors—
No—yet still stedfast, still unchangeable,
Pillow'd upon my fair love's ripening breast,
To feel for ever its soft fall and swell,
Awake for ever in a sweet unrest,
Still, still to hear her tender-taken breath,
And so live ever—or else swoon to death.

Love Poem 1
This poem is not a personal appeal but a universal definition of love, which the poet defines as constant and unchangeable in the face of any circumstances. It is like the North Star, he says, which, even if we don't know anything else about it, we know where it is, and that's all we need. Even death cannot lord itself over love, which persists to the end of time itself. The final couplet strongly reaffirms his commitment:

> If this be error and upon me proved,
> I never writ, nor no man ever loved.

The problem is that if Shakespeare is right about love's constancy, then none of the other poems in this list would have been written, or else they're not really about love. It seems Shakespeare may be talking about a deeper layer of love, transcending sensual attraction and intimacy, something more akin to compassion or benevolence for your fellow man. In this revelation of the nature of such a force, from which common love is derived, lies Shakespeare's genius.

Let Me Not to the Marriage of True Minds (Sonnet 116)

by William Shakespeare (1564–1616)

Let me not to the marriage of true minds
Admit impediments. Love is not love
Which alters when it alteration finds,
Or bends with the remover to remove.
O no! it is an ever-fixed mark
That looks on tempests and is never shaken;
It is the star to every wand'ring bark,
Whose worth's unknown, although his height be taken.
Love's not Time's fool, though rosy lips and cheeks
Within his bending sickle's compass come;
Love alters not with his brief hours and weeks,
But bears it out even to the edge of doom.
    If this be error and upon me proved,
    I never writ, nor no man ever loved.

Contributing Poets, Writers, and Editors

Anderson, C.B. was the longtime gardener for the PBS television series *The Victory Garden*. Hundreds of his poems have appeared in scores of print and electronic journals out of North America, Great Britain, Ireland, Austria, Australia, and India. His collection *Mortal Soup and the Blue Yonder* was published in 2013 by White Violet Press.

Bryant, Susan Jarvis is a church secretary and poet whose homeland is Kent, England. She is now an American citizen living on the coastal plains of Texas.

Dachstadter, Neal is a poet living in Tennessee. A member of the Demosthenian Literary Society at the University of Georgia, he deployed to Hawija, then wrote on Lookout Mountain, continuing with Delta Kappa Epsilon International. Berkeley, Ann Arbor, and Athens encouraged him as a writer.

Davis, Lorna is a poet who is happily retired and living in California. She can be reached at lornadavispoetry@yahoo.com

Dashiell, Michael lives in central Indiana. Throughout his long writing career he's had poems published in a variety of publications. Other than this, he's done seven books with Amazon. He's active on Facebook and Twitter, and has also founded a website: literaryzone.org

Foreman, Amy hails from the southern Arizona desert, where she homesteads with her husband and seven children. She has enjoyed teaching both English and music at the college level, but is now focused on home-schooling her children, gardening, farming, and writing. Recently, she has launched a blog of her poetry, The Occasional Caesura: A Pause Midline, at theoccasionalcaesura.wordpress.com

Geller, Conrad is a mostly formalist poet, a Bostonian now living in Northern Virginia. His work has appeared widely in print and electronically.

Grein, Dusty is an author, poet, and graphics designer from Federal Way, Washington. When he is not busy writing, he donates a great deal of his time and graphics talent. In honor of his grandson Eddy, lost to SIDS at 13 weeks old, he creates free memorial images for bereaved families, with a special focus on infant and pregnancy loss. His blog, From Grandpa's Heart, is followed by fans around the world.

Hodges, Ron L. is an English teacher and poet who lives in Orange County, California. He won First Place in the Society of Classical Poet's prestigious annual poetry competition in 2016.

Jackson, Bernard M., poet and reviewer, is based in England. Bernard has six poetry collections to his credit.

Karthik, Nivedita is a graduate in Integrated Immunology from the University of Oxford who likes reading books and traveling. She is an accomplished Bharatanatyam dancer and has given many performances.

Lefkowitz, Joshua won the 2013 Wergle Flomp Humor Poetry Prize, an Avery Hopwood Award for Poetry at the University of Michigan, was a finalist for the 2014 Brooklyn Non-Fiction Prize, and won First Prize in the 2016 Singapore Poetry Contest. His poems and essays have been published widely, and he also recorded humor pieces for NPR's *All Things Considered* and the BBC's *Americana*.

MacKenzie, Joseph Charles is the first and last American to win First Place in the Long Poem Section of the Scottish International Poetry Competition, Henry M. Austin Poetry Prize. Mackenziepoet.com

Mantyk, Evan teaches history and literature in the Hudson Valley region of New York. He is president of the Society.

McGrath, Reid is a poet living in the Hudson Valley in New York. He won First Prize in the Society's 2015 Poetry Competition.

Munsell, Mike writes riddles for Riddle Earth, a website he co-founded. His day job is with Greentech Media, where he writes about renewable energy.

Narayana, Sathya, once a lawyer, joined the government of India as Inspector of Salt in 1984 and got two service promotions. In May 2014, he took voluntary retirement as Superintendent of Salt.

Phillips, Connie is a former English teacher and editor living in Massachusetts.

Sale, James FRSA is a leading expert on motivation, and the creator and licensor of Motivational Maps worldwide. James has been writing poetry for over 40 years and has seven collections of poems published, including most recently *Inside the Whale*, his metaphor for being in a hospital and surviving cancer, which afflicted him in 2011. He can be found at www.jamessale.co.uk and contacted at james@motivational maps.com. He won Second Prize in the Society's 2015 Competition.

Shook, Don, former president of the Fort Worth Poetry Society and founder of The Actors Company, is a writer, actor, director, and producer. He has performed in theater, film, and television across the country, including opera at Carnegie Hall in New York, and as resident performer at Casa Manana Musicals in Fort Worth and Six Flags Over Texas in Arlington. He is an award-winning author who recently published novels *Bluehole* and *Detour* and four poetry books, and was selected 2009 Senior Poet Laureate of Texas. Don Shook Productions offers shows ranging from murder mysteries to musical reviews: www.shookshows.com

Simon, Michelle Tamara was born in Chicago, Illinois, and now lives in Scottsdale, Arizona. She writes poetry, essays, short stories, and fiction novels. Her first novel, *Hear of Malice*, was published in 2015 under the pen name C. Billie Brunson.

Smallwood, Carol has published over four dozen books, including *Women on Poetry: Writing, Revising, Publishing and Teaching* on Poets & Writers Magazine's list of Best Books for Writers. *Water, Earth, Air, Fire, and Picket Fences* is a 2014 collection from Lamar University Press; *Divining the Prime Meridian* is forthcoming from WordTech Editions. Carol has founded and supports humane societies.

Spencer Spragins, Elizabeth is a linguist, writer, poet, and editor who taught in North Carolina community colleges for more than a decade. She writes in traditional poetic forms that focus on the beauty of landscapes and their inhabitants. An avid swimmer and an enthusiastic fiber artist, she lives in Fredericksburg, Virginia.

Thompson, G.M.H. is a singer and rhythm guitarist. His poem, "Let Us Go," won the Winter 2016 Heart & Mind Zine Judge's Choice award in the poetry category.

Wyler, E.V. "Beth" grew up in Elmont, New York. At 43, she obtained her associate's degree from Bergen Community College. She and her husband, Richard, share their empty Fair Lawn, New Jersey, nest with three cats and a beta fish. Her oldest daughter is a biomedical engineer, and her other two children are SUNY undergraduate students.

Made in the USA
Las Vegas, NV
01 August 2021